ROUTLEDGE LIBRARY EDITIONS: LIBRARY AND INFORMATION SCIENCE

Volume 90

SERIALS INFORMATION FROM PUBLISHER TO USER

SERIALS INFORMATION FROM PUBLISHER TO USER

Practice, Programs and Progress:
Proceedings of the North American Serials
Interest Group

Edited by
LEIGH A. CHATTERTON AND
MARY ELIZABETH CLACK

LONDON AND NEW YORK

First published in 1988 by The Haworth Press, Inc.

This edition first published in 2020
by Routledge
2 Park Square, Milton Park, Abingdon, Oxon OX14 4RN

and by Routledge
52 Vanderbilt Avenue, New York, NY 10017

Routledge is an imprint of the Taylor & Francis Group, an informa business

© 1988 The Haworth Press, Inc.

All rights reserved. No part of this book may be reprinted or reproduced or utilised in any form or by any electronic, mechanical, or other means, now known or hereafter invented, including photocopying and recording, or in any information storage or retrieval system, without permission in writing from the publishers.

Trademark notice: Product or corporate names may be trademarks or registered trademarks, and are used only for identification and explanation without intent to infringe.

British Library Cataloguing in Publication Data
A catalogue record for this book is available from the British Library

ISBN: 978-0-367-34616-4 (Set)
ISBN: 978-0-429-34352-0 (Set) (ebk)
ISBN: 978-0-367-43135-8 (Volume 90) (hbk)
ISBN: 978-0-367-43153-2 (Volume 90) (pbk)
ISBN: 978-1-00-300151-5 (Volume 90) (ebk)

Publisher's Note
The publisher has gone to great lengths to ensure the quality of this reprint but points out that some imperfections in the original copies may be apparent.

Disclaimer
The publisher has made every effort to trace copyright holders and would welcome correspondence from those they have been unable to trace.

SERIALS INFORMATION FROM PUBLISHER TO USER: PRACTICE, PROGRAMS AND PROGRESS
Proceedings of the
NORTH AMERICAN SERIALS INTEREST GROUP

**3rd Annual Conference
June 4-7, 1988
Oglethorpe University
Atlanta, Georgia**

Leigh A. Chatterton
Mary Elizabeth Clack
Editors

The Haworth Press
New York • London

Serials Information from Publisher to User: Practice, Programs and Progress: Proceedings of the North American Serials Interest Group has also been published as *The Serials Librarian*, Volume 15, Numbers 3/4 1988.

© 1988 by The Haworth Press, Inc. All rights reserved. No part of this work may be reproduced or utilized in any form or by any means, electronic or mechanical, including photocopying, microfilm and recording, or by any information storage and retrieval system, without permission in writing from the publisher. Printed in the United States of America.

The Haworth Press, Inc., 12 West 32 Street, New York, NY 10001
EUROSPAN/Haworth, 3 Henrietta Street, London WC2E 8LU England

Library of Congress Cataloging-in-Publication Data

North American Serials Interest Group. Conference
  (3rd : 1988 : Oglethorpe University)
  Serials information from publisher to user.

  Bibliography: p.
  Includes index.
  1. Serials control systems—Congresses. 2. Serial publications—Congresses. I. Chatterton, Leigh. II. Clack, Mary Elizabeth. III. Title.
Z692.S5N67   1988   025.3'432   88-32871
ISBN 0-86656-894-8

Serials Information from Publisher to User: Practice, Programs and Progress

CONTENTS

Introduction *Leigh A. Chatterton* *Mary Elizabeth Clack*	xi
The Economics of Journal Publishing: A Case Study *Graham Marshall*	1
Copyright: Broadening Our Horizons *Brian D. Scanlan*	23
Copyright from the Perspective of Information Users and Their Intermediaries, Especially Librarians *Ben H. Weil*	27
Royalty Payments for Photocopying in Companies and Other Organizations *Donald W. King*	41
Copyright Clearance Center, 1988: A Progress Report *Virginia Riordan*	43
Copyright and the Scowling Publisher/Library Interface *Patricia H. Penick*	55
Photocopying and Copyright Problems for Colleges and Universities *John Marshall*	63
Accessing Electronic Journals: A Survey of Canadian and American Libraries *Ann Okerson*	73

ADONIS and Electronically Stored Information:
An Information Broker's Experience 85
    Constance Orchard

Serial Article Identifiers—SISAC, BIBLID, NISO, ISO,
ANSI and ADONIS: A Confusion of Alphabet Soup 93
    Sandra K. Paul

The Challenge of Cataloging Computer Files 99
    Anna M. Wang

Fatal Assumptions: Is There Light at the End of the Serials
Tunnel? 117
    Katina Strauch
    Mary Fugle
    Michael Markwith

An Overview of Current Developments in the Bibliographic
Control of Serials 133
    Ed Jones

WORKSHOP SESSION REPORTS

Serials Pricing: The Impact of Exchange Rates and Currency
Trends 141
    Cindy Hepfer

Getting Started with the USMARC Format for Holdings
and Locations 145
    Daphne Hsueh

Serials Snags, or, What to Do with Unsolicited Receipts
and Partners in Serials Access: Cooperation Between
Technical and Public Services 149
    Marjorie E. Bloss

Research Methods for Analyzing Serials Budgets 153
    George Lupone

Automated Binding Control: Libraries, Binders and Serial
Agents 157
    Martin Gordon

Automated Invoice Processing Using Vendor-Supplied Tapes 161
  Joseph Raker

Re-Automation of Serials Control: From OCLC's Serials
  Control Subsystem to INNOVACQ 165
  Karen Sandlin Silverman

Is There Life After Serials? 169
  Eleanor I. Cook

Introduction

The North American Serials Interest Group (NASIG) held its Third Annual Conference at Oglethorpe University, Atlanta, Georgia, from June 4-7, 1988. Our goal this year was to attract more publishers to the conference, and, to this end, emphasis was placed on serials publishing. Panel presentations included: "Current Issues in Copyright"; "Electronic Publishing, the ADONIS Project and SISAC"; and "Fatal Assumptions: Is There Light at the End of the Serials Tunnel?" a panel wherein the relationships between librarian, publisher and vendor were explored. In addition, individual presentations were given on the economics of journal publishing, on the challenge of cataloging computer files and on current developments in the bibliographic control of serials. Eight workshops, covering technical processing, cataloging, pricing and budgeting, and career development topics, were offered and the reports on these sessions follow the papers in this volume. A lively summary session brought the conference to a close. Our sincere thanks to our speakers, workshop leaders and audience who participated so enthusiastically in the discussions.

L.A.C. and M.E.C.
July 1988

ANNOUNCEMENT OF NASIG CONFERENCE GRANT AWARDS

The North American Serials Interest Group (NASIG) is an independent organization bringing together many segments of the serials information chain to study and explore common interests, problems, and ideas. NASIG is currently seeking candidates for grants to attend the summer 1989 annual conference to be held in Claremont, California. Through the granting of these awards, NASIG desires to encourage participation in this information chain by students who are interested in some aspect of serials work upon completion of their professional degree.

GUIDELINES

SCOPE OF AWARD: Recipients are expected to attend the entire conference and submit a brief written report to NASIG (for potential inclusion in a *NASIG Newsletter*). Expenses for travel, registration, meals and lodging will be paid by NASIG. A one year student membership will also be included.

ELIGIBILITY: Students currently enrolled in any ALA accredited library school program and who have expressed an interest in serials and/or technical services work are eligible. Applicants may be full or part-time students in degree program status at the time of application. Equal consideration will be given to all qualified applicants, following standard affirmative action guidelines.

APPLICATION PROCEDURE: Applicants should request an official application form from: Ann B. Vidor, Serials Cataloging Department, Price Gilbert Memorial Library, Georgia Institute of Technology, Atlanta, GA 30332.

APPLICATION DEADLINE: March 1, 1989.

AWARD NOTIFICATION: Award recipients will be notified by April 15, 1989. A maximum of six grants may be awarded for 1989.

The Economics of Journal Publishing: A Case Study

Graham Marshall

I'm very pleased to be at my second NASIG conference, the Group's third. Looking through the list of delegates I can see that there are a few more publishers here this year than hitherto. This is a welcome development and can only help to build a better relationship and better understanding between publishers and librarians and vendors.

The title of my paper is "The Economics of Journal Publishing." At this point I really must confess to you: first of all, I am not an economist; secondly, although I am plainly British, I am not now a British or even European publisher; thirdly, I am not really a journal publisher in the scientific sense.

Currently I am running Butterworths Legal Publishers in Boston, although up until last December I was head of marketing for Butterworth Scientific in the UK. Butterworth Scientific publishes some 100 scientific, technical and medical journals from offices in Guildford and Boston. My defection is recent enough for me not to want to back down from this opportunity to speak, not, I hasten to say, in defense of British or European trade practices, but as an advocate of good sense.

My intention today is to describe and illustrate some of the issues that are involved in launching a new journal. Butterworth Scientific publishes a range of journals: bi-monthlies, monthlies, quarterlies. Some are published on behalf of societies and associations and some are wholly owned by Butterworths. We have been publishing a number of journals (*Fuel* for example) for forty years or more. By

---

Graham Marshall, President, Butterworths Legal Publishers, 80 Montvale Avenue, Stoneham, MA 02180.

© 1988 by The Haworth Press, Inc. All rights reserved.

giving this paper, I have one very simple intention—to dispel any misunderstandings about the way that journals are published and how publishers make profits from journal publishing.

It might be worth my explaining how I came to volunteer for this job. It was a direct result of hearing some of the papers given at last year's meeting. I do not mean to imply that any of the matters and issues raised last year were fundamentally wrong; they were not. On the contrary, many were well researched, well organized, well delivered, erudite and learned, but some lacked, to my mind, a fundamental understanding of the journal publishing business, concentrating as they did on one or two topical and contentious issues only. The result reeked of propaganda. And when is the propagandist most active? Shortly before or during a war.

Looking at this group's acronym last year, on the flight out of Columbus, I came up with what I thought then was a more appropriate name. NASIG might stand for "Non-American Serials Illicit Gains."

Here then is the reason I am here. I cannot teach many, or maybe any, of my publishing friends and competitors anything much about journal publishing. I am not really here to teach at all. I am no academic but a practicing publisher. It is my business to make money in a responsible manner (publishing books or journals or whatever); to make money for my masters, my staff and for myself. Along the way I may talk about the, some say, "illicit" gains made by some non-American serial publishers.

It matters little whether my masters are ultimately bankers or shareholders (mine happen to be the shareholders of Reed International). Whoever they are, they have a right to expect me to make a reasonable profit on their investment, or, failing that, to promise that I will make a profit by a mutually-agreed date and to deliver that profit when the day comes. If I fail to do that, it is reasonable to expect that I will be replaced by someone who will, and if they cannot, then maybe my masters will decide to call it a day, withdraw their funds and invest their money elsewhere. Incidentally, I recently heard of a new group of European publishers committed to profiting from journal publishing called "G.A.I.N.S." ("Gouge Americans by Inventing New Serials").

Seriously, this long preamble is to position myself in the librarian/publisher debate, not as a pacifist nor as a soldier of fortune, but as one who wishes to give peace a chance. I referred earlier to some of the papers delivered at last year's meeting. Checking the list of delegates again I see that many of last year's speakers are here; I hope they are present today. For anyone who did not attend any of the earlier NASIG conferences, I urge you to read the proceedings if you have not already done so. These were published in *The Serials Librarian*.

In recent years it has become common for publishers to refer to those librarians who protest most vociferously about publishing practices as "aggressive." We talk of the aggressive librarian. Well, I think that some of my colleagues are here on a peace mission so I venture to suggest that we be referred to as peaceful publishers. We'll see.

You might say that there is nothing particularly political or contentious about a paper on the "economics of journal publishing" and you'd be right. Journal publishing is an industry and a vocation for many who labor in it. Very few enter the business to get rich and very, very few have achieved great wealth. My paper may begin to explain why.

I intend to deal this morning with a "real life" drama in four parts:

—an idea for a new journal
—initial research
—proposal and business plan
—how results do not always live up to expectations

Along the way we may touch upon some of the difficulties that journal publishers face and what, in this particular case, Butterworth Scientific's response was to those problems. It is unlikely that any of the practices that I describe will differ radically from those of other commercial or not-for-profit publishers.

The journal I have selected is a real one but I have chosen to conceal its identity as it is still published. It may not be too difficult for the determined researcher to uncover the title.

Let us go back ten years, three years before I joined Butterworth Scientific. At that time Butterworth's sister company, IPC Science & Technology Press (now completely merged with Butterworth Scientific), was publishing journals almost exclusively. Perhaps the most successful of the 25 titles the company had at the time was a monthly journal called *Polymer*.

There had been in the '60s and '70s a tremendous growth of interest in the whole area of polymers, both the manmade variety and the naturally occurring biopolymers. This interest was evidenced by the growing subscription numbers to the journal and the quantity and quality of the papers submitted.

Indeed, such was the pressure on editorial space in the journal that in the early '80s a separate "rapid communication" journal had to be launched alongside the main journal.

Enough has been said and published about the so-called "twigging" effect within areas of scientific endeavor for most people to have accepted that the phenomenon exists. I certainly do not intend to go into details. Suffice it to say that ten years ago *Polymer* was a branch bursting with buds, each twiglet representing a burgeoning subspecialty. (See Figure 1.) In 1978, the company had two successful journals in related but discrete disciplines, *Composites* (launched in 1970) and *Polymer* (started in 1960). We perceived a need for a journal to cover the rapidly advancing area of microbiology, molecular biology and genetic engineering and their application in the area now known as biotechnology, and successfully launched *Enzyme and Microbial Technology* in 1979. The whole area of polymer science was becoming increasingly specialized and seemed to be dividing into two principal streams: synthetic polymer science and the study of biopolymers and "natural" macromolecules. *Polymer*, our journal, attempted (up until 1978) to cover all these areas. (See Figure 2.)

Our plan was to launch another journal that would cover biopolymer science leaving *Polymer* to cover the expanding research into synthetic polymers and their chemistry, physics and applications.

Early in 1978 one of our bright young managing editors, Stella Dutton, submitted a proposal to spin off a new publication from the journal, *Polymer*. Stella had done a considerable amount of research which culminated in a 24-page report addressed to the publishing director, Chris Rawlins.

The decision to launch a new journal is not taken lightly because the scale of investment, compared to, for example, publishing a new book, is so large. Chris had to present Stella's proposal, with his recommendation to go ahead, to the managing director of IPC

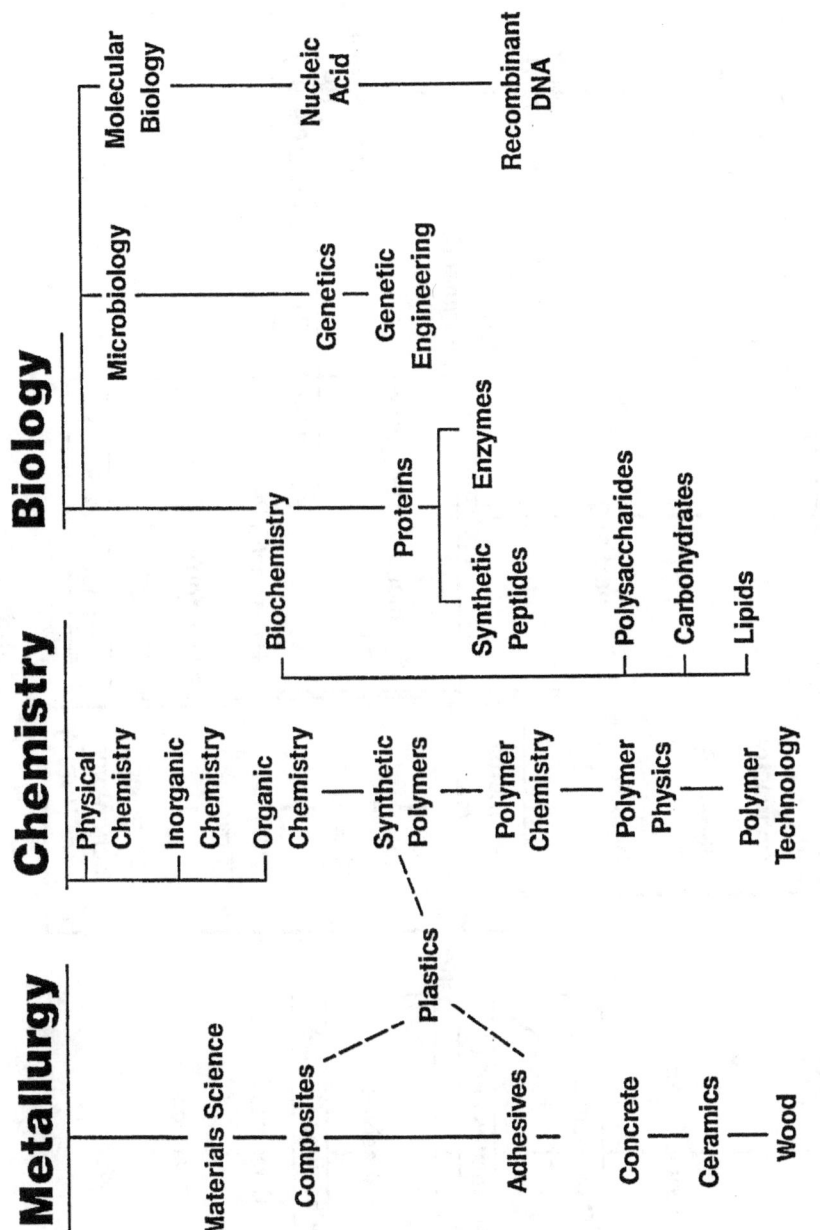

FIGURE 1

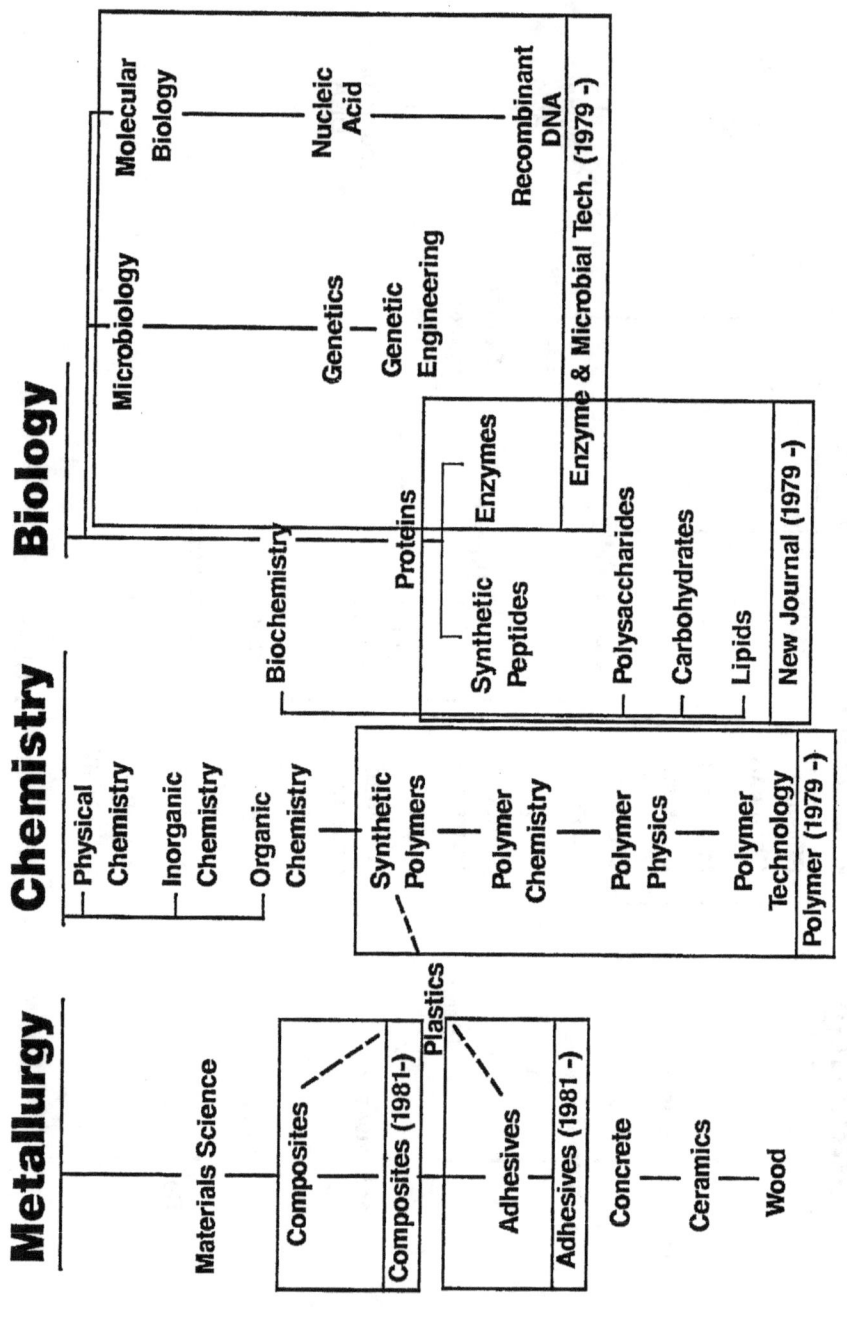

FIGURE 2

Science & Technology Press, who in turn had to obtain IPC Business Press Board approval.

The project looked attractive and the company had a proven track record of successfully spinning off new journals from existing ones, so the proposal was accepted and approved.

Let's return to the proposal for a moment and look at what it covered.

1. Background — A review of research activity currently taking place and anticipated in this field in all major regions of the world.
2. The perceived "need" for a new journal — why existing journals were unable to meet the needs of scientists working in this new discipline.
3. Content — It was proposed that the journal would contain: original research papers; short, rapid communication; commissioned review articles; book reviews; and calendar of meetings.
4. Contributors — It was intended that the journal would attract papers from biophysicists, biochemists, molecular biologists, physical chemists, and biomedical scientists.
5. Scope — A range of topics that might be covered was given together with titles of typical papers.
6. Editorial organization — potential candidates for the editorial board.
7. Format, frequency and price — A4 (11-3/4" × 8-1/4") was suggested, 48 pages plus cover, bi-monthly, £40.
8. Launch date — April 1979.
9. Competition — All the principal competing journals were listed and described, criticized and compared, although there were no direct competitors.
10. Upcoming meetings — a list of forthcoming scientific conferences covering areas relevant to the proposed new journal.
11. Launch countdown. (See Figure 3.)
12. Three-year business forecast — We'll be looking at these projections in detail in a moment.
13. Summary of market research — everything undertaken so far.
14. Promotion opportunities — mailing lists available or obtainable.

15. Sales forecast.
16. Geographical distribution—expected uptake in each of the major markets.
17. Direct mail program—priorities.
18. Relevant associations—with membership details.

On the 8th of June 1978, launch approval was given and the countdown to launch commenced in earnest. I won't attempt to guess at the cost involved up to that point: the editor, publishing director, marketing director, managing director, group board and their support staff had all been involved to a greater or lesser extent in the research and approval process.

First, let's consider the bare bones of Stella's proposal. (See Figure 4.)

Frequency—Although it is common to launch new journals on a quarterly basis, because of the anticipated flow of papers, we chose to launch bi-monthly. Thus, the publication is published frequently enough to be topical and to be seen to appear at discernible intervals and yet the page targets are not so stretching that the editorial board is unable to generate enough papers for the early issues (thereafter, if the journal has successfully identified a "niche," the papers should be largely self-generating).

Pages—This is, of course, related to frequency, page size and price. Typically, Butterworth journals are large format (11-3/4" × 8-1/4"), double column, which offers, we believe, the best scope for handling photographs, drawings, and statistical material. Forty-eight pages, plus cover, in this format was competitive with related publications (there were no direct competitors at that time) and in keeping with the anticipated flow of papers.

Price—Price setting is an art and not a science. I say this because it is not possible to come up with a formula for a new journal into which you can plug all the elements of costs and sales, and arrive at a single solution. Instead, there are a great many factors that have to be balanced when pricing a new journal; cost is certainly a major one but so is the price of competitive journals, any perceived price ceilings, and with a

PROPOSED COUNT-DOWN TO LAUNCH

1978

May	Go/no-go decision by Business Press
May	Potential Editorial Board members contacted
May	Direct mail list building
May/June	Editorial Board meeting
June	First brochure designed and printed and printed
August	Direct mail, promotion and soliciting for papers
September	Promotion at the Bristol Conference and at the 6th International Biophysics Congress, Tokyo
October/November	List building and direct mailing continues; advertising in relevant house journals. Also mailings jointly with Polymer
November/December	Refereeing and revision of papers

1979

January/February	Intensive mailing featuring pre-launch offer
February	Copy to printer
March	Page proofs received; First issue passed for press
April	Launch of first issue

FIGURE 3

Three Year Prediction

	79/80	80/81	81/82
Cum. Av. Sales	£ 350	£ 600	£ 750
Printed Pages	312	360	360
Sub. Price	40	45	50
Subs Revenue	12,352	22,783	31,900
Total Revenue	£12,352	£22,783	£31,900
Salaries	£4,969	£6,094	£6,633
Staff Expenses	500	600	700
Contents	2,400	2,400	2,400
Other Expenses	200	200	250
Total Editorial Costs	£8,069	£9,894	£9,983
Printing	£4,032	£5,221	£5,967
Paper	1,152	1,492	1,939
Total Production Costs	£5,184	£6,713	£7,906

FIGURE 4

new launch, how soon you expect or need to break even. All of these factors interact and so quite often the advice of a group of people involved with the journal is taken before a figure is arrived at.

Subscription sales — The number of expected sales in the first year can never really be accurately estimated. One can make educated guesses based on experience with related journals, size of market, anticipated market share, etc. Price, naturally, will have an effect, as will the nature and extent of the planned marketing campaign.

Looking at the journal in question, it was expected to be 48 pages, bi-monthly, and £40/year. Sales in the first year were rather optimistically pegged at 350.

Let's now take a look at the business plan contained in the launch proposal. Taking each element in detail:

Revenue — This is planned on a spreadsheet which plots the growth of the subscription base month by month. At the end of year 1, an average of 350 sales (including 100 at a special pre-launch rate) were projected. When I refer to sales, I am talking about total sales: subscriptions and back issues.

As it happened, the company's fiscal year ran from April to March so launching in April, there would be a full 6 issues in the year 1979/80, giving a total revenue of £12,352.

Salaries/staff costs — This line refers to in-house editorial staff costs. It was anticipated that the journal would require: 10% of Stella Dutton's time; 50% of an assistant editor; and 15% of a secretary.

Contents — This includes all the costs related to the editorial advisors whose job it would be to arrange the refereeing of papers, advise on editorial policy and direction, encourage submission of papers and suggest review articles for commissioning.

Printing and paper — These costs are self-explanatory, including: typesetting; printing, and binding.

I am sure everyone here realizes that most journal publishers do not simply print the quantity of each issue necessary to fulfill immediate subscription requirements (Figure 5a). It is important to maintain sufficient stock of back issues to satisfy claims and the demands of subscribers who do not commence their subscriptions until some time after launch and wish to buy back to the first issue. There is usually, in addition, a limited market for single copies, particularly of "special" issues. This figure shows the breakdown of the print-run of a typical Butterworth journal (see Figure 5b). All our back issue sales happen to be handled by Dawson and we and they attempt to keep copies of every issue of every volume (that we have published) in stock.

Circulation promotion — These are the direct costs (i.e., not including staff costs) attributable to this journal: printing and mailing brochures; display advertising; conference attendance, etc. Not included here but vital to the success of a new journal are: the pre-launch promotion costs, likely to be at that time around £2,000-£2,500. (See Figure 6.)

Distribution costs — They include the cost of maintaining the subscription records (handled by a bureau at that time) plus, of course, the costs of physically distributing the journal.

All of the above costs combined give the total costs figure which, when subtracted from revenue, produce this journal's contribution to profit.

Profit contribution — "Profit" is a bit of a misnomer, particularly with a new journal. In any case with any journal, there are a lot of overheads to be covered before contributions can be made to profit:
 a. *Development* — research and planning, pre-launch marketing, for this and other journals.
 b. *Management* — management and administrative costs.
 c. *Overheads* — cost of offices, rent, light, heat, telecommunications, insurance, etc.
 d. *Production staff* — at that time production staff costs were counted as an overhead and "promotion" as an attributable cost. Recently this has been reversed and production staff costs are allocated to each journal whereas promotion is taken as an overhead.
 e. *Promotion staff* — Salaries and overheads.

Analysis of Print Order - Quarterly Journal

MONTH	TOTAL SUBS	U/K SUBS	O/S SUBS	USA SUBS
APR MAY JUN	520	62	291	167
JUL AUG SEP	460	55	258	147
OCT NOV DEC	480	58	269	153
JAN FEB MAR	540	65	302	173

FIGURE 5a

Analysis of Print Order - Quarterly Journal

MONTH	FREES (INC VOUCHERS)	RESERVE	DAWSONS	TOTAL PRINT ORDER
APR				
MAY				
JUN	146	334	200	1,200
JUL				
AUG				
SEP	123	417	200	1,200
OCT				
NOV				
DEC	168	352	200	1,200
JAN				
FEB				
MAR	145	315	200	1,200

FIGURE 5b

Three Year Prediction

	79/80	80/81	81/82
Circulation Promotion	£3,500	£3,000	£2,500
Distribution	480	858	1,152
Total Direct Costs	£17,233	£20,465	£21,541
Profit Contribution	(4,881)	2,318	10,359
% Contribution	(40%)	10%	32%

FIGURE 6

To cover all these overhead costs, as a rule of thumb, a journal in Butterworth is expected to contribute at least 30%. Other publishers will have differing requirements. In the proposal from which these figures have been taken, the projection for year three indicated a profit contribution of 30%. History shows however that in years one and two, the profit contribution was well below the required level and, in any case, as we shall see, this projection turned out to be optimistic in several respects.

The figures in this launch proposal were in fact modified before launch and a more modest sales forecast of 200 used for the business plan which was finalized in December 1979. (See Figure 7.)

It is Butterworth's practice to record and monitor both subscription numbers and total sales. Because subscribers may elect to commence their subscriptions at any time during the year, the number of paid subscriptions varies issue by issue. It is therefore quite useful to look at the cumulative average of total sales in the financial year in question.

Editorial costs proved to be higher than proposed and sales lower than projected. These two factors combined to worsen the financial outlook. In fact, at the end of the first year, sales were running at 89, well below even the revised plan. By the end of the second

Subscription Sales and Total Sales

	APR	MAY	JUN	JUL	AUG	SEP	OCT	NOV
Total Sales	259		287		304		283	
Cum Av Sales	259		273		283		283	
Subscriptions	241		257		269		271	

FIGURE 7

year, the figures had risen to 200 but by then, other difficulties were beginning to emerge. Right from the launch it was clear that there would be no shortage of papers, quite the reverse. The problem was, by Volume 2, affording enough pages in the journal to publish sufficient material to make an impact on the rapidly growing backlog of papers awaiting publication.

It is self-evident that the more pages you publish the greater your costs. By July 1980, 15 months after launch, the backlog amounted to 61 unpublished, accepted contributions with a further 21 being refereed or revised. A related problem concerned the broad spread of subjects being submitted. Far too many papers were right on the fringe of the planned scope of the journal. This could be tracked to the structure of the editorial board which had no single chief. This problem was resolved by appointing a senior controlling editor.

So, just into its second volume, the journal was facing two major crises. Firstly, far from being in the business of rapid communication, publication time was running at 10/12 months because of the backlog. Issue sizes and therefore production and distribution costs were running over budget. To keep total costs within reason, the promotion budget was being squeezed. Secondly, subscription numbers were much lower than expected although we were seeing record numbers of reprint requests, often as many as 300-400 of one paper. This raised some concerns that researchers wanting information that had been published in the journal were getting the papers from the author free of charge. Promotion had also generated considerable interest. Of the 500 sample copy requests generated in year one, only 43 subscribers could be traced as a result. It is notoriously difficult to track and measure the results and effectiveness of subscription sales promotion. Certainly, you can track both the number and geographical spread of sample copy requests, but, because so often the individual interested in receiving the journal (who sees the sample copy) is not the person who actually acquires it, monitoring is nearly impossible. Some tough decisions needed to be made:

- Whether, when and for how long to increase issue sizes.
- Whether to stop throwing good money after bad and to close the journal.
- Whether to sell the journal — but, would we find a buyer?
- Whether to relaunch — not really valid, as evidence indicated that the journal was on the right track editorially, if a little unfocused.
- Whether to re-absorb the journal back into *Polymer* — could work but would need the backing of the editorial board.
- Whether to publish the journal as an additional section of *Polymer* or include it in the Polymer subscription — too risky because potentially damaging to *Polymer* subscriber base.

It was in fact decided to publish larger issues (64 pages plus cover) and even one at 88 pages to reduce the backlog of papers, using staff and production savings and cuts in promotional expenditure to keep the journal within budget limits.

At the next annual price review, a major price increase was agreed to as necessary to support the increased issue size. Fortunately, this had no discernible effect on subscription growth, which, although very slow, was steady.

Nine years later, the journal is still being published and issues are regularly 64 pages. Average sales are running just under 300 and the price is £152 UK and £175 overseas. That's an average annual, "compound" increase of 15%!

In that period Butterworths and IPC Science & Technology Press merged and the format and construction of the business plan documents have changed, so that some items previously counted as overhead are now included as costs and vice versa. Nevertheless the principal elements remain the same.

The figures we'll be looking at (Figure 8) are in fact from the 1988/89 business plan, that is the twelve months beginning April 1988. As we go through them, it might be worth making a comparison with the original pre-launch projections.

The price has increased fairly dramatically from £40 for the UK in 1979 to £152 in 1988. Eighty-six percent of subscribers are overseas and the overseas rate has increased just as much from £104 to £175. It might be worth pointing out that Butterworths has opted to price all its scientific journals in the currency of origin so that jour-

88/89 Budget

	(1988)	(1989)
Price UK	152.00	162.00
Price OS	175.00	187.00
Price US	175.00	187.00
Subs UK%	0.14%	38
Subs OS%	0.86%	266
Cum. Av. Total		275

FIGURE 8

nals published in the UK are priced in pounds sterling and those published in the US are priced in dollars. (I decided to address the difficulties being experienced by librarians in North America and elsewhere a couple of years ago. Butterworth's solution was to withdraw from the chancy and unpopular system of speculating on pound/dollar exchange rates. Dollar prices were originally introduced to make the purchase of British journals *easier* in the US but this necessitated fixing an artificial rate as much as a year before new prices were announced. The publicity given to the problems caused to the library market by a weak dollar need no rehearsal here, but suffice it to say that there were problems for the publisher, too. For a journal published in the UK, although 80-90% of sales are made outside of the home market, usually 100% of the costs are in pounds sterling. So, electing to price our UK journals in pounds and our US journals in dollars enable us to budget more accurately.)

Subscription numbers seem to be level at 275 after nine years compared to the *first* year's projection of 350. Costs have nearly doubled from £17,233 to £32,394 but the make-up of costs has changed (Figure 9). The size of the journal is now 64 pages compared with 48 pages. Revenue has gone from £12,352 to £46,513 (Figure 10). So there is now a contribution of 14,119 or 30 percent. The journal is, after nine years, in a position to contribute, in a modest way, to profits and not just to overheads (Figure 11). This journal is one example; Butterworths and other journal publishers will have many more, some successful and some less successful.

Inherently, there was nothing wrong with the journal:

— It was spun-off from a very successful title
— Active area of research
— Plenty of good quality papers
— Other related publications in the list
— High profile and active editorial board
— Interdisciplinary appeal
— Stable subscription base

But it did suffer from one major weakness: lack of subscriptions, which led to high price and poor profitability.

In its early years there were also some difficulties with speed of

88/89 Budget

Costs	
Edit. Salaries	4,459
Product Cost	10,872
Contributors	6,072
Edit. Freelance	4,800
Illus. Fees	600
Illus. Salaries	319
Reprints	658
Prod. Sundries	120
Carriage	1,734
Subs Records	774
Prod. Salaries	1,986
Journal Directs	32,394

FIGURE 9

publication because of the volume of publishable material and the impossibility of fitting it into the budgeted issue sizes. In the end, all the problems were addressed and by dint of some good management and some tough decisions (in the face of what was at the time a highly unionized workforce), the journal was saved. In-house staffing had to be reduced by withdrawing the shared editorial assistant and making use of the secretary working with the outside editors to handle the flow of correspondence with contributors. Illustrations were used as provided by the contributor instead of being redrawn. Promotion spending was cut back. The quality and in particular the coverage of papers was reviewed and the editorial board restructured in order to focus the journal more tightly, and of course, the price was increased substantially.

It is my belief that there will be an increasing number of journals in this position. Scientific research continues and its pace shows no sign of slackening. The various disciplines and specialties continue to branch out and "twig" into subspecialties. New journals are

88/89 Budget

Revenue

Subscriptions	44,817
Advertisements	0
Reprints	1,096
Singles/Backs	600
Journal Revenue	46,513

FIGURE 10

88/89 Budget

Journal Contrib.	14,119
% Contribution	30%

FIGURE 11

needed as fora for the exchange of ideas and information in these new areas.

Most of my publishing colleagues present will have experienced difficulties with new launches. The period before breakeven is ever lengthening and any publisher whose journals are not breaking even or are *only* breaking even will soon be out of business. At one time, this period was three years. Recently one might allow five years. Journals launched in 1988 may take *seven* years before they are covering overheads and contributing to profit. Why is this? Not lack of interest from those who need to read these new journals; the number of reprints and sample copy requests tells us that. No, it is an understandable caution on the part of librarians who have a key role in the acquisition process. There seems to be a wait-and-see attitude: that is, wait until a volume or two has been published before registering a subscription. This phenomena is evidenced by increasingly low subscription start-up numbers and increasingly high back issue sales figures. The effects of a massive increase in resource sharing and legalized copying of individual articles also contribute to the lengthening of the breakeven period.

This phenomena is not restricted to commercial publishers. Exactly the same market conditions apply to not-for-profit organizations. It is also worldwide. The spiral of cancellations, copying and resource-sharing is a particularly vicious circle.

It struck me forcibly when I sat in the audience at last year's NASIG conference that our business, the information business, must be in dire straits if a serious and committed professional group is meeting to discuss the very real problems of diminishing library funds and the difficulties of collection management in the current economic climate *but* most of the opportunities to seek solutions to these problems were missed.

The combined might of librarians, vendors, publishers, and academics may . . . just may be able to draw public attention to the shortage of funds available for research, for library collection development. If we're all too busy fighting each other, we will make no headway at all.

Well, I promised you a talk about the economics of journal publishing. I cannot conclude my presentation without giving a plug for one of my company's publications, *Journal Publishing*, by Gillian Page, Robert Campbell, and Jack Meadows (Butterworth). This book will tell you a lot more than I can about the whole business.

Copyright: Broadening Our Horizons

Brian D. Scanlan

NASIG has grown up considerably over the last three years and our annual meetings have reflected this growth. During our 1988 session we addressed the issue of copyright for the first time. This development is an important one because we finally explored a key factor—photocopying—in what has been the chief issue to date—serial pricing. Extensive photocopying has in part contributed to the erosion of journal subscription levels and to higher journal prices. Our discussion ranged from the question of copyright transfer to the Copyright Clearance Center's (CCC) site licensing of university libraries.

Transfer of copyright from the authors of articles in scholarly journals became widespread practice after the 1976 Copyright Statute. (The owner of the copyright of this introduction and other articles in this issue is Haworth Press.) Librarians have described what on its face may seem like an "unfair" information chain. A researcher, usually in a university, produces an article, and transfers the right to that information to a publisher; the researcher's university library, then in turn is "forced" to repurchase that information from the publisher. Why not then, as Stephen Breyer has suggested (Breyer, 1970, 281-351) eliminate copyright entirely: as soon as the article is published, it should be considered public domain. In a utopian world, that set-up would work fine. No one, after all, would come upon what would be the perfectly legal business of

---

Brian D. Scanlan, Senior Editor, Elsevier Scienca Publishing Company, Inc., 52 Vanderbilt Avenue, New York, NY 10017.

Address reprint requests to Elsevier Science Publishing Company, 655 Avenue of the Americas, New York, NY 10011.

reprinting a journal issue the day after it is published and selling for lower price. And if someone did reprint material, commercial publishers would quickly be out of business, and much more of the information now dispersed would not be distributed at all (Asser, 1987, 9).

Too often high-level scientific publishers are thought of as mere purveyors of information. The better publishers, however, enhance and improve the information they distribute. Stringent refereeing, which results in rejection of many articles and, for those accepted, in revisions for accuracy and clarity, line-editing, typesetting, printing, and organized, regular distribution adds value to researchers' material. In this sense, then, authors are being reimbursed for their work, if not in an outright financial fashion. The system requires investment from the publisher, for personnel, printing, and distribution, and generally speaking, the higher the investment, the higher the "value-added." As Patricia Penick of the IEEE points out, new technologies, such as CD-ROM, are requiring operational restructuring and even higher financial commitments on the part of the publishers. These new technologies, she writes, "are considered necessary to provide appropriate access to users of . . . information. None would be possible without the . . . ownership of copyrights."

Each of the following articles provides an overview of one aspect of copyright. Ben Weil, who has been very influential in informing our understanding of copyright, discusses the 1976 Copyright Statute and the subsequent problems of interpretation, especially by librarians. He notes that copyright will become even more complicated with the advent of inexpensive scanners which will allow for easier input of information into large-scale electronic storage and retrieval systems. Virginia Riordan, of the CCC, presents a history of the organization, how it works, and an update of its current activities. As of the end of 1987, some 1,300 foreign and domestic publishers had registered more than 100,000 titles with CCC. About 2,400 organizations and individuals had opened accounts with the CCC by year-end 1987, and 48 site licenses were in effect. Last year, the CCC entered into discussions with several major universities and publishers to explore academic site licensing, which means that many NASIG members will probably be more affected by its activities in the future. In her paper, Patricia Penick, IEEE's director of intellectual property rights, provides a frank discussion of different points of view that publishers and librarians take when it comes to copyright. The last article is by John Marshall, assistant vice president for legal affairs at Georgia State University. Whereas librarians have often been faulted for their lack of education regarding copyright, John rightly points out that some publishers' unreasonable permission requirements or inexpediency in dealing with such requests can make it difficult for librarians and users of material to comply with the law.

Copyright and compliance with copyright law are becoming even larger issues because new technologies are making it possible to access the same information through a variety of routes. Publishers, faced with declining institutional subscription bases, will be keeping a close eye on the information resources they provide and how those resources are being accessed. NASIG, which already has copyright on its agenda, is in a good position to serve as forum for helping to formulate policy as the issue of copyright reaches beyond large companies and copyshops into libraries. "In the future," Ben Weil notes in his article, "Both librarians and publishers have more to gain from cooperation than from confrontation, and their stress should be on ethics and empathy." That's good advice for all of us as we discuss copyright at upcoming NASIG meetings.

REFERENCES

Asser, P.N. (1987). Photocopying here and now. *Rights*, 1(3): 8-11.

Breyer, S. (1970). The uneasy case for copyright: a study of copyright in books, photocopies, and computer programs. *Harvard Law Review*, 84 (December): 281-351.

Copyright from the Perspective of Information Users and Their Intermediaries, Especially Librarians

Ben H. Weil

SUMMARY. Because of fair use, individuals making single-copy photocopies of copyrighted material are seldom directly concerned with copyright. Librarians, the chief suppliers of copies, are given many exemptions in the Copyright Statute, but under a multiplicity of conditions. The Statute is not a model of clarity, especially for industrial libraries. In the future, both librarians and publishers have more to gain from cooperation than from confrontation, and their stress should be on ethics and empathy. This paper attempts to clarify some of the copyright aspects still in question, especially since technological developments will introduce further complications.

Copyright, specifically the U.S. Copyright Statute, has meant different things to different groups at different times. To the Congress in session after the adoption of the Constitution, and to subsequent Congresses, it has been one mechanism for implementing an important power permitted to it under the Constitution (Article 1, Section B):

> The Congress shall have the power . . . to promote the progress of science and the useful arts, by securing for limited times to authors and inventors the exclusive rights to their respective writings and discoveries.

Ben H. Weil, Information Center Manager, EXXON (retired), 4 Wells Lane, Warren, NJ 07060.

© 1988 by The Haworth Press, Inc. All rights reserved.

To authors and their publishers, it has been the shield with which to protect their creations so that future works might be funded. Especially in this age of technology users of copyrighted materials and their intermediaries, librarians etc., have come to see copyright as interposing new cost barriers to the accessing of knowledge.

Before I address some copyright issues that may be of interest, let me hasten to say that I am not exactly a librarian. I was educated as a chemical engineer, but before I retired I was chiefly a manager of industrial research information centers that usually included libraries at their core. I am also not an attorney. Hence, I do not pretend to practice copyright law in this paper. However, I *am* an information area professional who has been intimately involved, for over three decades, with many of the copyright matters that concern librarians. So, perhaps what I present here will be useful. (I have also included some bits of history, by way of explanation, and some philosophy, mine and others.)

DIRECT USERS OF PHOTOCOPIES

Direct users of photocopies, those desirous of obtaining information from convenient-to-use photocopies of articles which appear in issues of serials that the users do not own and which cannot be given them to keep, are seldom directly concerned about copyright. The users want these copies quickly, and for some decades now have received them. Many of these users know that there are copyright limitations on their making or using multiple copies of given documents without permissions or royalty payments. Few personally concern themselves about this. (I wrote about some aspects of this a few years ago in a paper entitled "Why Should Chemists Care About Copyright?"[1]) Moreover, when it comes to their own copying, at least some individuals have heard that under the Copyright Statute (Section 107, "fair use"), they are entitled in many instances to make single photocopies for their own use. Publishers, however, believe that this privilege is strictly limited to individuals in for-profit organizations. When it comes to obtaining copies, attention to copyright matters has usually been delegated, by default, to the librarians or other information-center people to whom users turn to provide the needed copies.

COPYRIGHT ROLE AND PROBLEMS OF LIBRARIANS

Most librarians, ill prepared by what little they were taught about copyright in library schools, turn to the outpourings on the subject from their library associations. Occasionally, they seek the advice of their organization's general or patent counsels, few of whom are very knowledgeable about copyright. Yet, publishers' views on the subject are often given short shrift, as being self-serving. To put it succinctly, not enough librarians know about the basic informational publications available from the Copyright Office.

The major library associations, to some of which I belong, have long been active in the copyright area. In the more than twenty years in which the 1976 Copyright Statute was under debate, these associations vigorously fought for the legal right to continue to make single photocopies for library users without payment. Since they and their users represent an important and large constituency and since their purposes are often for the benefit of the public the library associations won many special exemptions. Nevertheless the rights and needs of other participants in the communication continuum, authors, publishers, creators, and initial distributors of the works being copyrighted had to be considered also, the victories were by no means complete. They were hedged in by the kinds of statutory verbiage deemed necessary for legal clarity.

Unfortunately, soon after the passage of the Copyright Statute some of the library associations rushed guidelines to the statute that in places went well beyond its dictates and intent into print. Newer guidelines are usually much more accurate in their interpretations, but some damage was done. How does one erase what has been written and read? Also, the major library associations, embittered by pre-statute struggles, and presumably not desirous of limiting in any way what they had gained, have been largely unwilling to discuss even the meanings of certain common words that suddenly became statutory terms, "systematic" and "concerted." Some of these terms are semi-defined in the reports of the branches of Congress, but not very clearly. As a result, many problems of interpretation go unresolved for practicing librarians seeking to comply with the statute.

Many new librarians cannot understand how the Copyright Statute could be unclear on library matters after twenty and more years of prepassage debate and countless conferences among librarians and publishers. What many of the present generation do not realize is that this statute froze into law many library-related specifics on which the publishing and library communities had not reached complete understanding. After a long delay caused by disagreements, the statute was passed very quickly when agreement in an unrelated area, cable television, was finally reached. In the rush to hold on to this cable television agreement, resolution of library area uncertainties and remaining disagreements were not deemed important enough to Congress to hold up passage of the statute. Guidelines for "Photocopying—Interlibrary Arrangements" developed by CONTU (the National Commission on New Technological Uses of Copyrighted Works) were rushed into Congress' Conference Committee Report[2] at the last moment. These guidelines were Congress' understanding of the meaning and exemption limits of the Copyright Statute's Subsection 108(g)(2).

Space considerations do not permit discussion of all the points still at issue, but the following examples should be informative.

PHOTOCOPYING IN INDUSTRIAL LIBRARIES

When the Senate passed its copyright-revision bill in 1975, the committee report that accompanied this[3] clearly said, with examples, that the special exemptions granted to libraries in Section 108 were intended "to preclude a library or archive in a profit-making organization from providing photocopies of copyrighted materials to employees engaged in furtherance of the organization's commercial enterprise, unless such copying qualifies as a fair use, or the organization has obtained the necessary copyright license."

The copyright bill passed by the House of Representatives in 1976 did not change the related language in Section 108. The accompanying report of the House Committee on the Judiciary[4] did not disagree with the Senate's interpretation if the for-profit organization's library program was for "'multiple' or 'systematic' photocopying." The House report then went on to say that "Isolated spontaneous making of single photocopies by a library in a for-profit organization, without any systematic effort to substitute photocopying for subscriptions or purchases, would be covered by [permitted by] Section 108, even though the copies are furnished to the employees of the organization for use in their work. Similarly, for-profit libraries could participate in interlibrary arrangements for the exchange of photocopies as long as the production or distribution was not 'systematic'." The chief for-profit prohibitions were sale of the photocopies, the making or distributing of multiple photocopies, and "if the photocopying activities were 'systematic' in the sense that their aim was to substitute for subscriptions or purchases."[3]

One would have thought that the matter was finally resolved by the House-Senate Conference Committee. While the committee did not change the statutory language, it did say in its report that in regard to "the meaning of 'indirect commercial advantage,'" as used in Section 108(a) (1), in the case of libraries or archival collections within industrial, profit-making, or proprietary institutions:

> As long as the library or archive meets the criteria in Section 108(a) and the other requirements of the section, including the prohibitions against multiple and systematic copying in subsection (g), the conferees consider that the isolated, spontaneous making of single photocopies by a library or archives in a for-profit organization without any commercial motivation, or (the) participation by such a library or archives in interlibrary arrangements, would come within the scope of Section 108.[4]

Nevertheless, the debate goes on because neither the House nor the Conference Committee made any changes in the language of the pertinent portions of Section 108 as drafted by the Senate Committee. In addition, there is legal precedence in such cases for the meaning of the language provided by its originator, the Senate. The ink was hardly dry on the Copyright Statute before the chairman and counsel of the Senate Committee pointed this out, even though it appears not to have been mentioned during either house's passage of the Conference Committee's report. Other arguments on this point were published in 1982 by Charles Lieb, then copyright counsel to the Association of American Publishers[5] and by Elmer and

Hornick, who present a somewhat less restrictive view on inhouse copying.[6]

PHOTOCOPIES OR SUBSCRIPTIONS

Librarians have long since recognized that much of the language of Section 108 in the Copyright Statute concerns attempts to prohibit or limit the substitution of photocopies for subscriptions. Further, librarians, and many enlightened publishers have also recognized that for many purposes subscriptions are not meaningful or practical whereas photocopies can be. For example SDI alerting and online searching of extensive bibliographic databases would include several thousand journals. Few or no libraries can be expected to subscribe to all or even most of these journals. Yet, individuals now call on libraries for access to many of the articles from these several thousand journals.

Some of these photocopies would inevitably have to be provided beyond the limited Copyright Statute exemptions. Consequently the wording of Section 108 would seem hopelessly archaic had not the Senate Committee also recommended in its 1975 report that "concerning library photocopying practices not authorized by this legislation . . . workable clearance and licensing procedures (should) be developed." The establishment of the increasingly useful Copyright Clearance Center was a direct response to this Senate pronouncement. Unfortunately, some major library associations are at best still lukewarm about the CCC. Their long standing no-fee for library services orientation still seems to inspire opposition to copyright-royalty fees.

MAKING MULTIPLE PHOTOCOPIES

It seems abundantly evident from Section 108 of the Copyright Statute that its photocopying exemptions *do not* extend to the making or distribution of multiple photocopies. Strangely, most libraries (70+%, from a King Research study) do not seem to be complying with this statutory requirement. Here, at least, there is no room for interpretory misunderstanding: the Copyright Statute does not permit permission-free making of multiple photocopies of copyrighted documents except in a limited way for classroom use.

Since multiple subscriptions are rarely a practical substitute, the Copyright Clearance Center's programs can again be useful. The making or obtaining of multiple copies from CCC-registered serials may be accomplished by reporting and paying the stated fees (Transactional System), or by having paid the appropriate CCC licensing fee required of for-profit companies (Annual Authorization Service).

INTERLIBRARY-"LOAN" PHOTOCOPIES

The library/publisher debate over the provision for interlibrary-loan photocopies, instead of actual document loans, was one of the most prolonged during the period when the Copyright Statute was being developed. The debate was so prolonged that the aforementioned CONTU Guidelines barely made it into the Conference Committee's report. In essence, the guidelines say that a library meeting the qualifications and observing the restrictions of Section 108 (which I will summarize later) may obtain, within a given year, up to five photocopies of articles published during the last five years of a given serial, if they keep appropriate records.

The limit of "five" represented quite a library victory. Indeed, it is quite probable that the publishers did not clearly understand that this would permit fee free, about 90% of the then prevalent interlibrary-loan single-copy photocopying. The CONTU guidelines left undefined the limit for interlibrary photocopying from journals more than five years old. This is still a subject for argument. For a time after the guidelines adoption debate raged over whether the "five copies" was an absolute maximum or a "minimum" that could be exceeded in certain cases. For example, could a last request for three copies of an article which would total seven copies for a year for a given serial be fulfilled within the bounds of the statute?

REPRODUCTION BY LIBRARIES AND ARCHIVES

I have referred repeatedly in this paper to the requirements and privileges afforded to libraries by Section 108 of the Copyright Statute, but I have so far touched on only some of these. What follows is a summation of Section 108 taken from a feature article on "Copyright Basics and Consequences"[7] which Barbara Friedman Polansky and I wrote in 1984. (Internal quotation marks surround direct quotations from the Copyright Statute's Section 108.)

Congress added section 108 to the Copyright Statute because it felt that "reproduction by libraries and archives" merited some privileges that go beyond those of fair use, but that these privileges should have definite limitations. However, as we have seen the complications introduced by some of the terminology has led to misunderstandings and debate.

> Section 108 permits a library or archives to produce or distribute a single copy of a work in its collection if this is done "without any purpose of direct or indirect commercial advantage"; if its collections "are open to the public" or available "to persons doing research in a specialized field" as well as to affiliated researchers, and if the copy "includes a notice of copyright". A damaged, lost, or stolen copy may be duplicated in facsimile form "if the library or archive has, after a reasonable effort, determined that an unused replacement cannot be obtained at a fair price".
>
> Under Section 108, a library or archives may make for a user, or may request in his behalf from another library or archives "no more than one article or other contribution to a copyrighted collection or periodical issue . . . or a small part of any other copyrighted work". However, the copy must become the property of the user, and the library or archives may prepare or obtain it only when it "has had no notice that the copy or phonorecord would be used for any other purpose than private study, scholarship, or research" and when "a warning of copyright", as prescribed by the Register of Copyrights, is displayed "where orders are accepted" and is included on the

library's order form. Moreover, with the same provisos, a copy of an entire work or a substantial portion of it may be requested "if the library or archives has first determined, on the basis of a reasonable investigation, that a copy or phonorecord of the copyrighted work cannot be obtained at a fair price".

A library or archives is not liable for what is done at unsupervised reproducing equipment located on its premises, provided that a notice is posted "to the effect that the making of a copy may be subject to the copyright law". An individual using such equipment or requesting a photocopy from the library or archive can be held liable "for copyright infringement if his act . . . or later use . . . exceeds fair use as provided in Section 107".

Library photocopying under Section 108 is further restricted to "isolated and unrelated reproduction of a single copy or phonorecord of the same material on separate occasions". The right to do such copying "does not extend to cases where the library . . . or its employee—(1) is aware or has substantial reason to believe that it is engaging in related or concerted reproduction or distribution of multiple copies or phonorecords of the same material, whether made on one occasion or over a period of time, and whether intended for aggregate use by one or more individuals or for separate use by one or more individuals or for separate use by the individual members of a group; or (2) engages in the systematic reproduction or distribution of single or multiple copies or phonorecords . . . : *Provided*, That nothing in this clause prevents a library or archives from participating in interlibrary arrangements that do not have, as their purpose or effect, that the library or archives receiving such copies or phonorecords for distribution does so in such aggregate quantities as to substitute for a subscription to or purchase of such work".

Section 8 also states that its provisions do not extend to musical works, graphic works, motion pictures, etc. It concludes with the proviso that, every five years after 1978, the Register of Copyrights shall prepare and submit to Congress a report on the extent to which Section 108 "has achieved the intended statutory balancing of the rights of the creators and the needs of users" and that this report should also include recommendations for any legislative changes needed to solve any problems that may exist."*

I have deleted from this quotation the article"s material on the CONTU guidelines that would have duplicated information which appears earlier in this paper, and also the otherwise duplicatory discussion of the Conference Committee"s pronouncements on copying by for-profit libraries.

Readers will have noted the multiplicity of now-statutory terms that are open to various legitimate interpretations. What, for example, is a *reasonable* effort to obtain an unused replacement of a damaged, lost, or stolen copy at a *fair* price as a prelude to duplicating one in *facsimile* form? One can only regret that the representatives of library and publisher associations assembled several years ago by David Ladd, the then Register of Copyrights, for a variety of copyright purposes, found themselves unable to develop such definitions.

FAIR USE, AND COPYING FOR EDUCATIONAL PURPOSES

Since Section 108 was drafted to give libraries exemptions which exceed those that might be available under ""fair use"" (Section 107) libraries usually need not depend on fair-use privileges. Nevertheless, libraries may occasionally have reason to use Section 107 in view of the fact that it is the statutory section that authorizes copying for educational purposes, an area in which educational/institutional libraries continue to play an important roll.

Section 107 codifies what previously had been judicial doctrine. It was not intended to change, narrow, or broaden judicial fair-use exceptions in any way. According to this section,

---

*Reprinted with permission from Reference 7, Copyright 1984, American Chemical Society.

the fair use of a copyrighted work, including such use by reproduction in copies or phonorecords . . . for purposes such as criticism, comment, news reporting, teaching (including multiple copies for classroom use), scholarship, or research, is not an infringement of copyright. In determining whether the use made of the work in any particular case is a fair use the factors to be considered shall include: (1) the purpose and character of the use, including whether such use is of a commercial nature or is for nonprofit educational purposes; (2) the nature of the copyrighted work; (3) the amount and substantiality of the portion used in relation to the copyrighted work as a whole; and (4) the effect of the use upon the potential market for or value of the copyrighted work.

The copyright-bill report of the House Committee on the Judiciary[4] included guidelines on classroom copying, in not-for-profit educational institutions, that were later accepted by both houses of Congress. These guidelines, however, were not a part of the Copyright Statute itself, any more than were the CONTU guidelines. Although they definitely pertain to what an educational library may do for teachers and students, they are too detailed for inclusion here. Academic/library associations disagree with the guidelines on the basis that they had no in-put into the drafting process. Yet, these same guidelines figured prominently in the settlement of a publisher copyright-infringement suit against New York University for copying beyond that permitted by the Copyright Statute.[8]

ETHICS; TACTICS; EMPATHY; INTENT

I have long respected and admired librarians for their devotion to user services, and their willingness to go beyond the call of duty to provide them. I have also understood their zeal to make their services and holdings broadly available, although I have considered their efforts to make all these available without charge unrealistic, albeit idealistic.

As an information-center manager, I have understood only too well that library budgets which fail for one reason or another to keep up with increasing costs, hamper the efforts of librarians to provide the collections and services needed by their users. It is only natural, then, that librarians and their associations oppose anything that unnecessarily or unfairly increases their expenses. Rightly or wrongly, compliance with the 1976 Copyright Statute has gotten a "bad rap" here. Until its passage, single-copy interlibrary lending had proceeded without limits other than those required by the lenders [and an ALA code]. As a result single-copy inhouse photocopying went on without any payments beyond subscriptions. Try as they might the library associations were unable to persuade Congress that publishers did not need to place limits on these practices in order to protect their necessary subscription revenues, or to be able to collect compensatory fees for levels of photocopying that would threaten it.

The many years of debate have taken their toll in bitterness, personal resentments, some "dirty tricks," and a cut-off-our-noses to-spite-our-faces unwillingness among library-association representatives to work further with publishers for mutual progress. For example, while the Copyright Clearance Center is finally progressing successfully, think how much more library oriented its programs would have been had the organized library community participated actively, as originally invited?

I could go on, but I would rather simply urge forgetting the past and seeking better cooperation for the future. Librarians and publishers have much to gain: by seeking better understandings of each others' copyright-area problems, as they long have in other areas; by being reasonable where fees are mandated (both in setting them and in striving to pay them); and in jointly working to master a technological future that may otherwise overwhelm them both.

Librarians must accept the fact that, for some legitimate reasons, certain dishes have disappeared from what was an entirely free lunch. With help from those who receive the resultant revenues, librarians must seek better funding to pay the "new" copyright-involved costs. Also, they must realize that such beneficial programs as networking and "resource sharing" will face copyright barriers that will not always be surmountable without copyright-related costs. The "buzz word" will have to be cooperation, not contention.

Changes in the Copyright Statute are hard to effect, and the two five-year studies and reports of the Register of Copyrights under Section 108 have not inspired concrete action. Indeed, the library community, as part of its present hold-the-line tactics, has not asked for such action. One must remember that it is the intent of the Copyright Statute, under Congress' Constitutional mandate, to balance the rights of creators with those of the public, including the services provided to the public by knowledge distributors such as publishers and librarians. Librarians know that they, publishers, and some others are parts of the same family—the information continuum.

For the present, the Copyright Statute is the law of the land. Better, more ethical, more empathetic efforts are needed to make it work optimally.

TECHNOLOGY

One last word, about the impacts of technology. Much is being done and written about individual computer workstations, online searching, downloading, CD-ROMs, electronic mailboxes, etc. Their impacts on libraries and publishers will be profound, as will their interaction with what we have been calling copyright. Something of this can be gleaned from two of my recent papers,[9,10] but I will not attempt to summarize them here. Suffice it to say that librarians and publishers will have many more common interests and problems in the future than they will have areas of conflict.

REFERENCES

1. Weil, B.H. Why should chemists care about copyright? *J. Chem Inf. Compt. Sci.* 22 (1982): 61-63.

2. U.S. Congress. House. Committee on Conference. *General Revision of the Copyright Law, Title 17 of the United States Code, Conference Report* [*To Accompany S.22*]. 94th Cong., 2d sess., 1976. H. Rept. 94-1733.

3. U.S. Congress. Senate. Committee on the Judiciary. *Copyright Law Revision, Report Together With Additional Views* [*To Accompany S.22*]. 94th Cong., 1st sess., 1975. S. Rept. 94-473.

4. U.S. Congress. House. Committee on the Judiciary. *Copyright Law Revision. Report Together With Additional Views* [*To Accompany S.22*]. 94th Cong, 2nd sess., 1976. H. Rept. 94-1476.

5. Lieb, C.H. *Document Supply in the United States*. Amsterdam: Scientific, Technical, & Medical Publishers (STM). STM Copr. Bull. 19.

6. Elmer, M.C. and Hornick, J.F. In-house photocopying subject to new challenges. *Legal Times* 5, no. 11 (1983): 11,14.

7. Weil, B.H. and Polansky, B.F. Copyright basics and consequences. *J. Chem. Inf. Comput. Sci.* 24 (1984): 43-50.

8. Wise, D. Guidelines set for photocopying material: publishers settle with N.Y.U. in copyright violation suit. *N.Y. Law J.* 189 (1983):1,3.

9. Weil, B.H. and Polansky, B.F. Copyright, serials, and the impacts of technology. *Serials Rev.* 12, no.2-3 (1986): 25-32.

10. Weil, B.H. The many routes to published information. *Schol. Publ.* 18 (1987): 263-70.

Royalty Payments for Photocopying in Companies and Other Organizations

Donald W. King

SUMMARY. The Association of American Publishers (AAP) has taken the position that all photocopying of journal articles in companies should be subject to royalty payment. Should this be true? Studies by King Research show that photocopies used by readers come from four basic sources: personal subscriptions, library (and office collection) subscriptions, separate copies requested by libraries from other libraries or document delivery services. This paper presents data concerning the extent to which such photocopying takes place and the likely economic implications of such photocopying on the revenue to publishers and to the companies. Suggestions are given for a system which achieves fair revenue to publishers, yet does not overburden companies or constrain reading by limiting amount of photocopying.

PAPER WAS UNAVAILABLE AT TIME OF PUBLICATION.

Donald W. King, President, King Research, Inc., 6000 Executive Blvd., Rockville, MD 20852.

Copyright Clearance Center, 1988: A Progress Report

Virginia Riordan

INTRODUCTION

The Copyright Clearance Center (CCC) was established by photocopy users, authors, and publishers in response to the expressed desire of the Congress that a service be created to facilitate implementation of the revised U.S. copyright law that took effect January 1, 1978. It is the only service of its kind in the U.S., operating a centralized photocopy authorizations and payment system. CCC assists users of copyrighted material in their efforts to comply with the law, as well as foreign and domestic copyright owners.

Nineteen eighty-eight marks CCC's 10th Anniversary. It has grown substantially from the handful of U.S. publishers who registered the initial 1,000 scientific, technical, and medical journals, to an international roster of some 1,300 participating publishing organizations with more than 100,000 books, journals, magazines, and newsletters listed. The few major corporations that obtained limited authorizations to photocopy through the copy-based transaction service in 1978 have expanded to forty-eight licensees (as of December 31, 1987) under the statistically based annual licensing service. The number of copies authorized through CCC in 1987 was 3,000 times the number cleared in 1978. Today CCC is a part of a thriving international federation of Reproduction Rights Organizations that provide authorizations to users and collect royalties for rightsholders across national boundaries.

Virginia Riordan is Manager of Marketing Support Services for the Copyright Clearance Center, 27 Congress Street, Salem, MA 01970. Her primary responsibilities include Publisher and User Relations and promotion.

© 1988 by The Haworth Press, Inc. All rights reserved.

What follows is a summary of CCC's activities to date, its programs and services, and new areas being explored.

ANNUAL AUTHORIZATIONS SERVICE

Development of the annual photocopy licensing program, the Annual Authorizations Service (AAS), was initiated in late 1981. It had become clear to CCC management that the Transactional Reporting Service was being utilized by only a fraction of the large organizations with significant needs to photocopy copyrighted material. Field interviews with executives of major corporations had yielded a startling consensus. While they agreed that copyright owners had a right to compensation for the copying of their materials, they declined to use the CCC transaction service. Objections to the administrative burden of training staff and establishing data-gathering procedures in order to report copying to CCC were commonly cited. So CCC began to develop, with the assistance of a major corporation, the licensing arrangement that ultimately became operational in late 1983.

The AAS provides a corporate-wide license to photocopy from all CCC-registered works for one year, and is renewable for an additional year at the licensee's option. The user makes a single payment to CCC to copy from participating publications, for internal use only. Distribution to third parties is expressly prohibited. The license authorizes copying of portions of works; and expressly prohibits copying of a book, journal, etc., in its entirety and entry into a database.

The need to record and report each copy made from participating publications, except for a brief copy survey period, is obviated under the AAS. Several statistical methods for collecting data are available to users, and represent the evolution of a more streamlined, less intrusive approach that remains statistically valid.

The initial data collection approach was based on a 90-day survey of copying activity at *all* U.S. locations owned and operated by a potential licensee. The 90-day results were multiplied by four to yield a projected annual copying level. As in the Transactional Reporting Service, publishers establish the copying fees for their titles. These individually-set copy fees, for each of their registered works identified in a survey, were then applied to the annualized copies' estimate and totalled, to yield the license cost. (It is important to note that all titles registered in the AAS are licensed to the user organization, whether or not they appear in the survey, and whether or not their fees are directly used in calculating the total license fee.)

The next data collection approach was the development by MIT and Harvard econometricians of a statistical model that allows for a copying survey to be conducted on a representative *sample* of a potential licensee's U.S. locations (typically 5-8 sites with 10-20% of total employees). Total copies company-wide were extrapolated from the sample data; an average price per copy (from the prices individually set by publishers) developed; and the coverage rate (ratio of CCC-registered copies to all copies of copyrighted works appearing in a survey) generated. The three factors were multiplied for each of the potential licensee's major business groups and totalled to yield the license cost.

An even more streamlined approach to data collection was implemented during 1987. Under this new method, a license can be created based upon pooled industry-wide copying data. Because the statistical collection coefficients (which are applied to each licensee's particular employee demographic configuration) are industry-based and not company-specific, a license can be priced and executed *before* the copy surveys are conducted. A limited survey of two sites is still required for distribution purposes, and to freshen the industry-based coefficients, but it need not occur prior to issuing a license. Increasingly, this approach is the one preferred by potential licensees.

Copying in the corporate environment that could be considered "fair use" is addressed in the design of the licensing system. Rather than have corporate employees make individual judgments as to copying acts during the survey period, each publisher may state, as a percentage, that amount of copying from a particular work that could be considered "fair use." This percentage is applied against the copying fee set by the publisher and acts as a discount on the fee.

At the end of 1987, 48 licenses, more than 2.5 times the number at the end of 1986 (19) were in force. Industries represented by the licensees include: aerospace, chemical, communications, electrical engineering, fuel, pharmaceuticals and publishing. Figure 1 depicts the tremendous growth in the number of licenses in force since the inception of the AAS in 1983. As a result, the number of copies authorized through the AAS collection base continued to climb — from almost 700,000 during 1986, to approximately 1.5 million during 1987, an increase of more than 100%.

TRANSACTIONAL REPORTING SERVICE

Since 1978 corporations, document suppliers, academic institutions and others have used the Transactional Reporting Service (TRS) to obtain authorizations to photocopy from registered publications and to pay requisite royalty fees. Publishers establish their own authorization fees (if any) for copying from their publications. Fees may be set in several ways: (1) a fixed base fee for the item to be photocopied, regardless of the number of pages in the item; (2) a per-page fee; and (3) a combination of a base fee plus per page fee. Serial publishers tend to use a fixed base fee (per-article fee) or base plus per page fee, while book publishers tend to use a per-page fee formula.

The *Publishers' Photo-Copy Fee Catalog* (PPC) lists participating titles and their respective copying fees. It is published in full three times per year and is a primary reference source for photocopy users of the service.

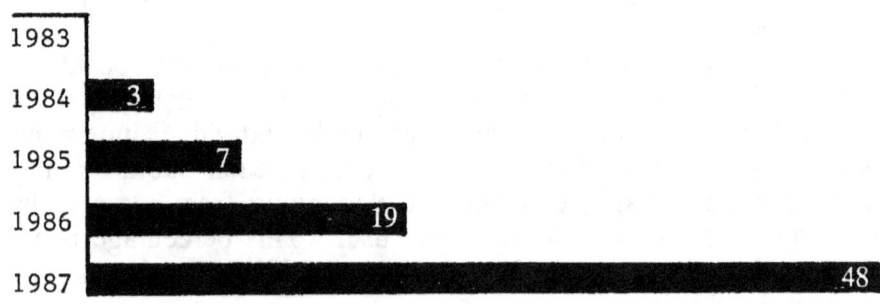

Figure 1.   LICENSES IN FORCE
ANNUAL AUTHORIZATIONS SERVICE

From 1978 to 1982, participating publishers of scholarly publications were required to print a unique CCC-fee code on the first page of each article in the publication. (The CCC article fee-code consisted of the standard number, year of publication, volume number and issue designation, first page number of the article, the span of pages of the article, and the author royalty indicator.) Publishers were also required to print a photocopy permissions statement in the front matter of the publication, outlining the scope of permissions granted through CCC and identifying their participation in CCC, near the masthead in the front of the publication.

During this time, publishers of trade or non-scholarly works (e.g., publications where the items most frequently copied are staff-written) were required to print a single serial-fee code following the permissions statement. (The serial-fee code contains the standard number, year of publication, and fee to photocopy an item [article, page, or chapter].)

In January 1983, CCC removed the requirement that publishers of scholarly works code each article and suggested that *both* scholarly and non-scholarly publications carry a fee-code once in the front matter following the permissions statement. User organizations' ongoing reluctance to report article-specific copying activity to CCC and the seeming lack of interest by publishers in obtaining article copying data (versus publication-based copying data) confirmed the modification.

To this day, many scholarly publishers continue to print individual fee codes on articles published in their titles. This is no doubt a result of having systematized the process of constructing and printing fee codes. However, they also recognize that a fee-code on an article is a clear indicator to a user that the work is registered with CCC and that a royalty is due for copying the item.

Under the transaction service, users record and report copying from participating publications. Four key data elements are provided to CCC: the publication title or standard number, year of publication, number of pages copied and the total number of copies made. A variety of methods may be utilized to report copying to CCC. The most frequently used method of reporting is the submission to CCC of an extra copy of the first page of an article that includes a printed fee-code, or an extra copy of the page in a publication that includes a printed permissions statement and fee-code. (In a serial, the statement and fee code are near the masthead; in a book, it is on the verso of the title page that contains copyright information.) Log sheets are also utilized, where users provide the data elements referenced above; reporting on magnetic tape is available to large-volume user organizations.

There is no charge to a user organization to register with CCC. Fees are billed only when copying is reported. Photocopy reports are processed monthly, and invoices for royalty fees are generated at that time. Special, cumulative reports of a user organization's copying activity for a specific time period are available to the user for a fee.

Full service (or Level I Service) is automatically provided at no charge to organizations that report 120 copies or more in a six month period. Level I Service includes account maintenance, updates of the PPC and copying data retained in the CCC database for one year. Full service may be purchased for $45.00/semi-annually by users who report more than 120 copies over six months.

Limited (Level II) service is automatically provided at no charge to all users who report less than 120 copies during a six month period. It includes monthly processing of photocopy reports. When accompanied by payment, single issues of the PPC may be purchased for $30.00 each, or an annual subscription may be obtained for $75.00. The PPC is also available to user organizations in machine readable form, for $1,200.00 per annual subscription.

Figure 2 graphically depicts the copies reported to CCC under both the transaction and licensing services. As the chart illustrates, the transaction service experienced consistent increases between 1978 and 1986. This growth occurred despite the conversion of several major accounts to the AAS in the years since 1984. However, in 1987 the number of copies reported decreased by 31% from the 1986 totals, reflecting the continuing transition of large volume accounts from the transaction to the licensing service. Through year-end 1987, approximately 3.5 million copies had been reported through the transaction service.

By the end of 1987, approximately 2,400 organizations and individuals had opened accounts with CCC: 768 were corporations, and document suppliers and others, comprising 32% each; 528 were

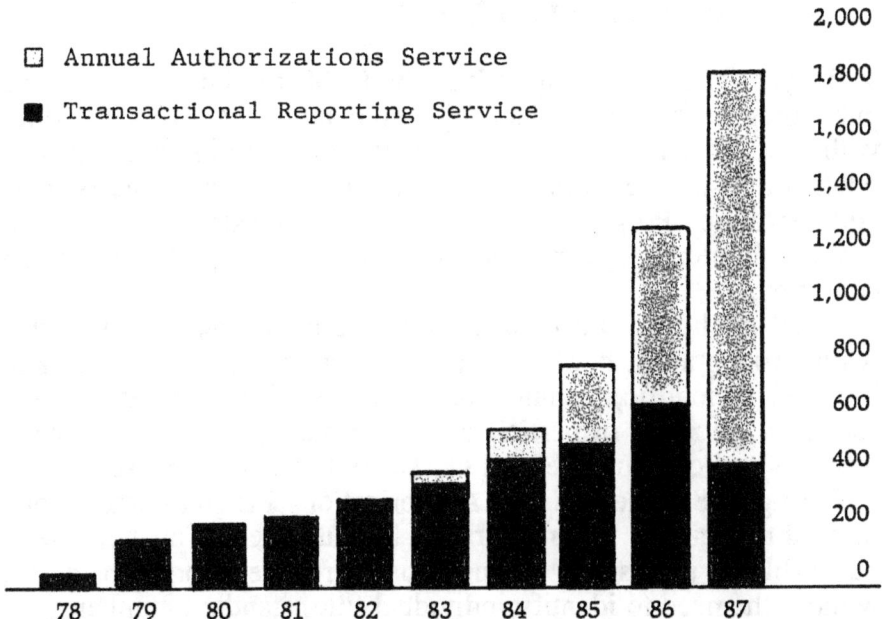

Figure 2. COPIES REPORTED TO CCC PER YEAR (IN THOUSANDS)

universities and colleges (22%); 168 were foreign organizations (7%); 72 were academic research libraries and 72 were government agencies (3% each); and 24 were public libraries (1%).

It is interesting to note that the copies reported by each group during 1987 were not related to the number of accounts. The distribution of reported copies was:

Corporations	55%
Document suppliers	35%
Academic reserach libraries, colleges, and universities	5%
Government agencies	1%
All others	4%

These percentages confirm prior years' activity levels.

PUBLISHER/TITLE REGISTRATIONS

By year-end 1987, approximately 1,300 foreign and domestic publishing organizations had registered more than 100,000 titles with CCC. Figure 3 shows the significant growth in the number of publications registered in recent years, a result of both the Blanket Authorizations Program and the en masse registrations of works through bilateral agreements with CCC-counterparts in foreign countries.

Serial publications accounted for 20% of the registered works, while monographs, books and proceedings comprised the remaining 80%. Scientific, technical and medical titles are heavily represented in the roster of participants, with the registration of general business and computer-related works continues to increase.

During 1987, the Blanket Authorizations Program was implemented to facilitate title registration by publishers. This new method enables a publishing organization to register works en masse, without the need to identify individual title, standard number, year of publication and copying fee data. Instead, a publisher provides CCC with its unique ISBN prefix, its standard fee for copying from

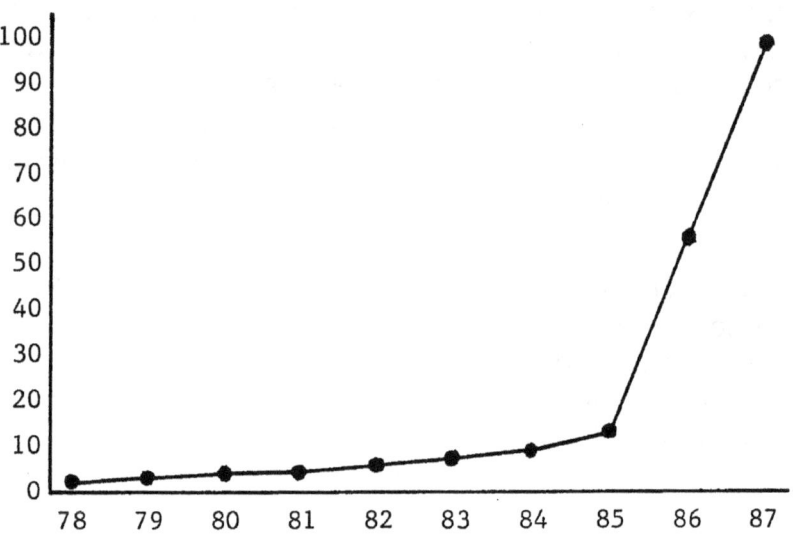

Figure 3. TOTAL NUMBER OF PUBLICATIONS REGISTERED (IN THOUSANDS)

the class of work, and a catalog of its publications (for reference purposes). The ISBN prefix is stored in the CCC computer. When a title and standard number which includes the publisher's unique ISBN prefix, is reported, authorization is granted automatically to the user and the appropriate fee billed. (A publisher may provide CCC with a list of works to be excluded from this system. This list is also consulted prior to authorization/billing.)

This particular blanket method facilitates book registrations. This does not apply to serials, which have no unique prefix that encompasses multiple titles. For serials, a publisher continues to provide specific title, ISSN, year of publication and copying fee data.

There is no charge to a publisher to register a work. However, a CCC service charge is deducted from the royalty-fee collected when a copy is reported. Under the transaction service, works with publication dates of 1983 to the present have a $.50 per copy processing charge deducted, while pre-1983 materials are processed at $.25 per copy. Under the license service, the service charge does not exceed 35% of the fees collected in the first year of a license, and not more than 25% in subsequent years.

DISTRIBUTIONS TO PUBLISHERS

After a three-year hiatus (1983 through 1986), CCC again began to distribute royalties collected to participating publishers. In March 1987, approximately $275,000 was disbursed to more than 250 participating publishers. This completed payment on copying from their publications reported by users of the Transactional Reporting Service during 1978, 1979 and 1980. (Partial distributions had been made earlier: 30% of 1978 copying fees, 40% of 1979, and 45% of 1980.)

As a result of collections during 1987, approximately $1,000,000, the single largest distribution in CCC history, was disbursed to 400 participating publishing organizations in March 1988. This completed payment for all copying of their materials reported by users of the TRS during 1981, 1982 and the first half of 1983. (Partial distributions of 22.5% of 1981 collections and 10% of 1982 had been made earlier.)

Copyright owners have granted authorization allowing CCC to use monies collected to cover its developmental and operating expenses. Individual agreements between publishers and authors govern the further apportioning of royalties. The Copyright Clearance Center's Board of Directors and management are committed to making distributions on a regular basis.

INTERNATIONAL

CCC has entered into agreements with five Reproduction Rights Organizations (RROs) in foreign countries: the Copyright Licensing Agency (CLA) of the United Kingdom, the Centre Francais du Copyright (CFC) of France, VG Wort of the Federal Republic of Germany, Kopinor of Norway, and the Copyright Agency Limited (CAL) of Australia. These agreements authorize CCC to collect on behalf of foreign rightsholders whose works are copied in the U.S., and users of CCC's Transactional Reporting Service and Annual Authorizations Service are authorized to copy lawfully from the thousands of titles owned by the foreign rightsholders.

Through the end of 1987, CCC was collecting royalties in the U.S. for over 750 foreign imprints. The number of publications authorized through these agreements has impacted significantly the titles available to U.S. users. Negotiations are underway with several other RROs, including Literar-Mechana (Austria), Stichting-Reprorecht (the Netherlands) and Prolitteris-Teledrama (Switzerland).

During 1987, CCC initiated the Foreign Authorizations Program. This program enables participating U.S. rightsholders to receive royalty payments for photocopying of their works overseas through agreements between CCC and foreign RROs. Within just three months of solicitation to join the program, approximately 50% of CCC-participating U.S. publishers had responded in the affirmative. Many view the program as their only practical means to obtain royalties on copying of their works in foreign countries. At its March 1988 meeting, the CCC Board of Directors ratified the first agreement under this program—a rights conveyance agreement between CCC and CLA of the United Kingdom.

It is important to mention that all of CCC's international agreements are based upon the principle of "national treatment," as found in the Universal Copyright Convention. In essence, fundamental fairness to all is insured by treating both foreign and domestic rightsholders comparably.

CCC is a founding member of the International Federation of Reproduction Rights Organizations (IFRRO), the international network for CCC and its counterparts. In late 1987, IFRRO reconstituted itself from an informal forum to a formal federation. As such, it will have standing to participate in relevant study groups and conferences of international bodies such as WIPO and UNESCO. (IFFRO's 13th general meeting was held in Boston in May 1987, and was hosted by CCC. The "Collective Administration of Rights in Computer Software" was the theme for the meeting, in which more than 45 organizations from 19 countries participated.)

The collective administration of rights and royalties through the cooperation of RROs is considered to be vital to the effective protection of publishers' and authors' rights worldwide. IFRRO will continue to be the primary agent for CCC in negotiating bilateral agreements and for discussion of collective licensing methods.

BUSINESS DEVELOPMENT/NEW MARKETS

In 1987, the Business Development Department was created to develop new programs to satisfy emerging copyright needs, while maintaining CCC's primary focus on expanding its corporate photocopy licensing program. Several areas are of keen interest: broadening the licensing program to other commercial entities; consideration/development of a licensing program for universities and government agencies; and consideration/development of a program to collect and distribute royalties for the copying of computer software.

During 1987, CCC began to market the corporate license program to law firms and to the financial sector, which includes banks, insurance companies, accounting firms and brokerage houses. Initial results are positive. Substantive discussions with several major universities and publishers to explore an academic licensing program took place in 1987. Issues surrounding the licensing of photocopying in the academic environment (e.g., fair-use, copy-shops, anthologizing) are complex and require creative solutions. However, all parties in the discussion agreed that there is a need for an easily administered method for universities to acquire authorizations for a broad range of textual material. It was also agreed that a comprehensive licensing approach, with CCC at the center and the university as licensee, is a practical way to address this need. Solution-oriented talks continue and the hope is to develop a pilot program by the end of 1988. Preliminary discussions with a government agency regarding licensing also took place in 1987.

In early 1988, the CCC Board of Directors approved the development of a pilot program to collect and distribute royalties for the copying of computer software. Market research to determine the feasibility of a program initiated in 1987, after extensive discussions with software publishers, users, and trade associations, indicated the desirability of a multi-publisher/title approach to the licensing of software copying. (Estimates of illegal to legal software copies in corporations and universities range from 1:1 to 3:1.)

Several key issues, however, will need to be addressed in the construct of the license: pricing, the need for common basic terms, multiple software products, and verification. Ongoing investigations are being conducted into the copyright implications of other current and emerging technologies, including electronic databases, hypertext, and new methods for electronic entry, storage, transmission, and utilization of print-generated material.

CONCLUSION

In its program development, CCC seeks to ensure that it will be able to assist rightsholders and users to convey authorizations and collect royalties efficiently and cost-effectively at a time when new technologies provide a myriad of challenges and opportunities to the protection of copyright.

REFERENCES

Alen, Joseph S. Successful Large-scale Photocopy Licensing in the USA. *Earth and Life Science Editing*, May 1985, 3-4.

Hoffman, Alexander C. and Eamon T. Fennessy. Testimony submitted on behalf of Copyright Clearance Center, Inc., at public hearings of the Register of Copyrights under the provisions of 17 U.S.C. 108(i), April 8, 1987, Washington, D. C.

Copyright and the Scowling Publisher/Library Interface

Patricia H. Penick

SUMMARY. The Institute of Electrical and Electronics Engineers, Inc. (IEEE) is the world's largest professional society and also a major world publisher. IEEE goes to considerable trouble and expense to hold copyright to its technical material both to protect and to be able to provide access to that material. Liberal reprint and republication policies, participation in the Copyright Clearance Center (CCC) and other efforts help ensure legitimate access. IEEE's commitment to the free flow of information does not, however, support the view that information must therefore be literally free. Unauthorized, unpaid for photocopying is a major concern. An environment which recognizes that copy machines are not free and that copy shops expect to be paid, but which gives short shrift to the intellectual property being copied, damages all in the information chain and should be of as much concern to libraries as it is to publishers like IEEE.

THE SCOWLING

Copyright is of major concern to most publishers. On the other hand, librarians seem to know little about it. Library schools rarely tackle even the rudiments of the subject. This discontinuity is, in fact, one reason—along with high prices for library subscriptions and varying titles for conference publications—why librarians and publishers, who should see themselves as part of the same information chain, instead scowl at one another. As viewed by one biased

---

Patricia H. Penick, Director, Intellectual Property Rights, Institute of Electrical and Electronics Engineers, Inc., 345 E. 47th Street, New York, NY 10017.

© 1988 by The Haworth Press, Inc. All rights reserved.

publisher (IEEE), a typical Librarian (L)/Publisher (P) dialogue might go something like this:

> **L:** All publishers do is provide the mechanism for ripping off authors at one end of the information chain and libraries at the other.
> **P:** Librarians don't know a thing about publishing. The review, selection, composition, printing and distribution needed to provide excellent journals to libraries and others require great professional expertise and is very costly.
> **L:** Publishers set enormous prices for library subscriptions and then have the gall to fuss about photocopying.
> **P:** Library subscriptions are intended for multiple use and are priced accordingly. Those prices don't, however, cover copying beyond the limits of the Copyright Law.
> **L:** Publishers seem to think libraries are ripping THEM off! Don't they know how much trouble it is to catalog their inconsistent output, to keep track of interlibrary loans and so forth? We post copyright notices all over our library copy machines. What more can we do? We're not responsible for what goes on down the street at the copy shop.
> **P:** Is it really possible that all library-related copying is Fair Use—or otherwise legal? From where we sit it looks like some libraries have become document delivery centers—and that can't possibly be fair.
> **L:** The mission of libraries and librarians is to promote the free flow of information. PERIOD.
> **P:** Information should certainly be freely accessible. That isn't to say, though, that information must always be literally free, i.e., without fee. Copy machines aren't free, and their use doesn't hamper the flow of information.

PROMOTING ACCESS TO INFORMATION

The Institute of Electrical and Electronics Engineers, Inc. (IEEE) is a not-for-profit professional society—the largest in the world—and publishes about 20% of the world's literature in electrotechnology. Although much of the information published is archival, most of it is of immediate utility and urgently needed by some subset or another of the electrical engineering and computer science community. Like most STM publishers, IEEE takes very seriously its obligation to provide access to the information in its vast array of journals, magazines, and conference publications. Holding copyright to all the copyrightable material it publishes is one way IEEE ensures appropriate access. Under the U.S. Copyright Law which took effect in 1978, copyright arises the moment a work is in tangible form. If a publisher doesn't arrange to have copyrights transferred, those rights reside with the individual authors or, in the case of "work made for hire," with the employers of those authors. Careful publishers like IEEE — and like Haworth Press — quite appropriately make publication contingent on the transfer of all copyrights. For IEEE, obtaining copyright to fifty thousand or so papers annually is a major undertaking. It's been especially difficult to wrest copyright away from the large corporations where many IEEE authors work. To do so, it has been necessary to convince corporate attorneys that, if IEEE holds all copyrights, as opposed to having them scattered among thousands of authors and other corporations, IEEE can then legitimately provide legal access to material authored outside their own corporations. IEEE is, of course, also able to protect the material on its own behalf as publisher, and also on behalf of the authors and the organizations for which they work. Once IEEE becomes the copyright holder, access to the copyrighted information is ensured in a variety of ways. For example:

Generous rights are immediately returned to authors and to their employers.

Liberal reprint and republication policies govern the several thousand permissions requests which flow into IEEE Headquarters annually.

IEEE belongs to the Copyright Clearance Center (CCC), thereby making it possible for information users like corporate libraries which also belong to CCC to photocopy legally the massive amounts of copyrighted information they need to do business and which otherwise would constitute copying beyond the limits of the law.

On the masthead pages of each IEEE serial publication, a statement appears saying that copying, by instructors, of isolated articles for traditional classroom use is permitted without fee. This policy, which is viewed even by other professional societies as giving away the store, is viewed by IEEE as an important contribution to education. It also recognizes in very practical terms an important symbiosis between the IEEE member who, as a professor, is both an author and a user of IEEE's published material. The policy has also made wresting copyright away from professors a relatively painless process! More seriously, IEEE's policy provides some relief for the Classroom Copying Guidelines which, though well intended, appear to some to be confusing or inappropriately limiting.

IEEE also permits photocopies of its papers to be sold through the University Microfilm Article Clearinghouse.

In the foreseeable future, IEEE expects to have its typesetters encode IEEE material into ASCII character sets using AAP/SGML standards so as to provide both traditional hardcopy and other products such as CD ROMS tailored to the needs of users. It's important to note that publishers who encode full text using the AAP/SGML standards will be able to provide very flexible, easily manipulated products which will be hardware and software independent. This will also provide the greatest possible compression, a non-trivial matter for librarians. For instance, if IEEE's 150,000 page annual publication output were simply put onto disks in pixels, i.e., compressed pictures, about fifty such disks would be needed. By encoding that same amount of material in ASCII, the number of disks is reduced to three.

The practices and plans described above represent a range of IEEE effort from a simple increase in "administrivia" to major operational restructuring and enormous financial commitments. All are considered necessary to provide appropriate access to users of IEEE information. None would be possible without the requisite ownership—in IEEE's case, the ownership of copyrights.

COPYRIGHT ABUSES

Even with its generous policies, IEEE shares the same concerns commercial publishers do about what appears to be rampant, illegal photocopying. IEEE isn't litigious and hasn't, and probably won't, participate in copyright infringement suits. However, IEEE is a member and strong supporter of the Association of American Publishers (AAP) which, in turn, has been involved in various actions involving illegal or questionable photocopying. A few such actions are noted below:

AAP has taken action in three cases involving university-related copying. Two were against off-campus copy shops. The third and most famous was against both New York University and the Unique Copy Shop.

Actions have also been taken against corporate libraries. The most famous, and still unresolved, is against Texaco. AAP has assured its members that the case will be pursued to completion despite Texaco's other problems.

AAP has filed amicus briefs in two cases in which the right of sovereign immunity granted to states under the 11th Amendment to the Constitution has been used according to AAP ". . . to subvert the integrity of copyright." The University of California at Los Angeles (vs. BV Engineering) won a lower court ruling that state officials were immune to liability for copyright infringement. AAP maintains that Congress didn't intend that states have carte blanche to violate the Copyright Act and is pursuing the matter at the appellate level.

AAP is presently gathering more data about photocopying. A copy shop will undoubtedly be one target. Another target for complaint is the British Library Document Service Centre (BLDSC, formerly BLLD), a major fill source for search systems like DIALOG. In a June 1, 1988 letter to Mr. Harvey Winter, Director of the Office of Business Practices, U.S. Department of State, AAP President Nicholas Veliotes says: "The Document Supply Centre of the British Library regularly engages in the unlicensed, systematic, massive-scale photocopying of (among other materials) STM journal articles for distribution to (among other groups) wholly commercial entities—both to profit-making corporate end users and to for-profit intermediate document delivery services for commercial redistribution to private, public, institutional and governmental users. The DSC engages in outright on-demand publishing activities. Yet it refuses to play by the rules of the game of any respectable publishing venture . . . and to obtain permission for its activities from copyright owners. . . ." The letter goes on to say: "The gall-ing fact is that U.S. commercial entities . . . are principal customers for DSC-made copies. Our members must not only suffer the theft of their intellectual properties abroad (in a "developed" country), but must endure the further indignity of having pirated copies thrown back in their faces across national boundaries. . . ." IEEE, despite its own liberal policies, is in accord that the copying problem cited is just as serious as the tone and content of this AAP letter indicate.

A FEW SMILES ALONG WITH THE SCOWLS

Amidst the copyright abuse and general chaos, there are a few bright spots. The Copyright Clearance Center really has achieved fiscal health. They recently sent IEEE a nice fat check. Their annual authorization program seems to be working, and they are now experimenting with publisher/university agreements to regularize university copying.

Many underdeveloped countries have, until recently, engaged in massive photocopying of copyrighted material almost turning such piracy into national industries. Thanks to the good work of AAP, Congress and the Administration have been persuaded to link the protection of publishers' intellectual property rights to U.S. trade agreements with the result that previously intransigient "pirates" now proudly proclaim adherence to good copyright practices. Overseas piracy may not be under control, but things are far better than they were, BLDSC notwithstanding!

Other countries which haven't worried much about copyright or which have old and clumsy laws are now recognizing the need to come to grips quickly with the increasing problems caused by electro-copying. Many countries with Reproduction Rights Organizations (RROs) have joined a new international body known as IFRRO (International Federation of Reproduction Rights Organizations). On one hand, a few of us light-minded souls suppress our giggles and wish the titles referred to "Reprographic Rights." On the other hand, the need for these organizations is urgent and welcome no matter what they call themselves.

One well-known copy shop appears to be regularizing its procedures and now can provide publishers with whom they have agreements with statistics on actual copying.

Interesting electronic document delivery experiments are being tried. University Microfilms has one. ADONIS, the born-again publishers' consortium, has another. Both use machine-encoded indexing, but compress "pictures" for their full text.

ONE FINAL FROWN

A potential threat to the modest gains in getting photocopying under control comes not from developing countries or even England, but rather from the Library of Congress. Dr. James Billington, the new Librarian of Congress, has let it be known that, among other initiatives, he'd like to expand the Library of Congress's optical disk experiment so as to be able to provide as much of the LC collection as possible electronically—on-site copying, documents delivered via telephone wires, etc.—to anyone anywhere who needs it. This is the free flow of information with a vengeance! Publishers are not amused. In a strong letter dated June 1 to Dr. Billington, AAP President Veliotes noted that "Wholesale copying or electronic full-text distribution or other uses without authorization would have a 'chilling' effect on authorship and creativity and would be resisted accordingly . . ." and that "AAP believes that while any such exploration of new directions may be timely, it should be undertaken in partnership with the private sector and reflect a particular sensitivity to the copyright concerns of American publishers. . . ." To attempt a little fairness, a representative from LC was asked at a mid-June meeting to comment on Dr. Billington's initiatives and indicated that they probably were not intended to be as all-encompassing as they appeared. Nonetheless, the threats of new technology whether from LC or elsewhere are very real. The publisher's view of the problem was eloquently summarized in the following brief quotation, again from AAP President Veliotes, in the Brace Memorial Lecture delivered in April 1988 at New York University:

Imagine a future in which one copy of a reference work, probably on CD-ROM diskettes, resides in a computer to which the whole world has dial-up access.

Using computers that exist today, hundreds of people could simultaneously "read" (and copy) the same part, or different parts, of the work. Obviously manufacture of the CD-ROM amounts to the making of a copy of the work and requires permission from the copyright owner. It must be clear that individuals with no relationship to one another, acting independently, who electronically peek at different portions of the work amount to "the public," that the Copyright Law covers such activities.

An equally serious electro-copying problem—where rights are clearer but enforcement remains difficult—is represented by the ability of users of such systems to copy, on demand, the extract that they have viewed, or even the entire work. Technology can assist here, provided that the designers and operators of the system make users accountable for their copying.

A FINAL SMILE

Despite any evidence to the contrary, most publishers in their better moments really do recognize that information has life after publication and that it is thanks to information professionals—librarians, for example—that this is so. For both librarians and publishers, the problems created by new technology burgeon and the solutions lag far behind. Tackling some of the problems together can only help. The forum provided by NASIG is an important step in the right direction. Maybe even in the RIGHTS direction as well.

Photocopying and Copyright Problems for Colleges and Universities

John Marshall

INTRODUCTION

In spite of an increasing awareness of the potential risk of copyright infringement as a result of multiple copying, college and university faculty members continue to use photocopies of journal articles and other published material for classroom teaching activities. In many courses there is a need for current and immediately updated information which may only be supplied by photocopying of recently published material. This photocopying, as a general rule, does not supplant the market for professional journals nor does it cause any realistic financial harm to publishers. However, much of the copying that is done for classroom use exceeds the minimum standards for fair use set forth in *The Agreement on Guidelines for Classroom Copying in Not-For Profit Educational Institutes*.[1] Although these guidelines purport to be the *minimum* standards of fair use, apparently publishers and some courts are looking to these guidelines to determine whether a particular use is fair use.[2] This potential conflict between the law and the needs of college and university faculty members places the serials librarian in a very difficult position. Quite often, multiple copies of journal articles are requested to be placed on reserve for classroom use or multiple copies may be requested through inter-library loan. This article will attempt to address these concerns and suggest an alternative for a more appropriate way of dealing with these copying issues.

John Marshall, Assistant to the Vice President, Georgia State University, 100 Decatur Street SE, Atlanta, GA 30303.

© 1988 by The Haworth Press, Inc. All rights reserved.

THE 1976 COPYRIGHT LAW
AND THE EXCLUSIVE RIGHTS
OF AN OWNER OF A COPYRIGHT

Article I, section 8 of the Constitution of the United States includes in the enumerated powers of Congress the power to "promote the progress of science in the useful arts, by securing for limited times to authors and inventors the exclusive right to their respective writings and discoveries." This grant of authority to Congress is the basis for the current copyright law enacted by Congress which is often referred to as the Copyright Law of 1976.[3] The dual purpose of the copyright law is to provide and disseminate information to the general public while at the same time to provide some remuneration to authors for the use of their work.[4]

There are five essential rights that a copyright owner has in his or her creation: (1) the right to reproduce the work, (2) the right to prepare derivative works, (3) the right to distribute the work, (4) the right to perform the work publicly, and (5) the right to display the work publicly.[5] Obviously, the photocopying of a copyrighted work is potentially in violation of the copyright owner's right to reproduce the work. As a general principle, unless there is some exception in the law which would allow an individual violating any of these exclusive rights the right to do so, there would be an infringement of the copyright.[6]

While there are several limitations under the Copyright Law on the exclusive rights of a copyright owner, there are two limitations in particular which should interest the serials librarian. First, section 108 of the law[7] sets forth certain rights of a library or archives to make copies of a work. Because faculty members often attempt to avoid the copyright problems inherent in making multiple copies for classroom use by placing journal articles on library reserve, it is important for the serials librarian, to examine this section. The law provides that it is not an infringement of copyright for a library or archives to make more than one copy of a work if:

1. the reproduction or distribution is made without direct or indirect commercial advantage;

2. the collections of the library or archives are either open to the public or available to persons doing research in a specialized field in addition to those researchers affiliated with the library;
3. the copy of the work includes a notice of copyright.

Further, subsection (d) of Section 108 provides that these rights of reproduction and distribution, of no more than one article or other contribution to a copyrighted collection or periodical, also apply to copies made from the collection of another library or archives if the copy becomes the property of the user. However, the library or archives must have no notice that the copy would be used for any purpose other than private study, scholarship, or research. Thus, it appears that making multiple copies of a copyrighted work to place on reserve for the use of students, would not fall within this exception. In fact, subsection (g) provides that if the library or archives is aware or has a substantial reason to believe that it is engaging in concerted copying of the same materials, then it is not protected under Section 108.[8] As a result, it may well be that section 108 does not cover any typical situation involving the photocopying of materials to place on library reserve. In fact, the former Register of Copyrights, David Ladd, in his report to Congress in 1983 stated that copying for reserve purposes is "not addressed by Section 108 . . . ."[9] Thus, it appears that a librarian must look to Section 107 and its provisions relating to "fair use" to determine the extent of copying which would be lawful when placing material on reserve.

However, there are other provisions of section 108 which may be important to the serials librarian. For example, subsections (b) and (c) authorize reproductions of published and unpublished works for purposes of preservation and security. If the work is a published work, such copying may be made to replace a copy which is damaged, deteriorating, lost, or stolen, if the library has determined that an unused replacement cannot be obtained at a fair price.[10]

FAIR USE AND SECTION 107

Since Section 108 may be of limited use to a faculty member or a librarian in attempting to establish the authority to make multiple copies of journal articles for use by students, it is essential that the provisions of section 107 be examined. Prior to the 1976 Act, the concept of fair use was created by the courts in order to allow certain uses of copyrighted materials notwithstanding the exclusive rights of copyright owners. Section 107 of the 1976 Act adopted the judicially created doctrine and set forth four criteria to examine to determine whether or not a particular use of a work is a "fair use." The four factors to be considered are:

1. the purpose and character of the use, including whether such use is of a commercial nature or is for non-profit educational purposes;
2. the nature of the copyrighted work;
3. the amount and substantiality of the portion used in relation to the copyrighted work as a whole;
4. the effect of the use upon the potential market for or value of the copyrighted work.[11]

In the case of *Harper and Row Publishers, Inc. v. Nation Enterprises*,[12] the Supreme Court of the United States analyzed carefully the defense of fair use. In this case, the *Nation* magazine had obtained a copy of the memoirs of former President Gerald Ford which were to be published by Harper & Row. The court examined the four statutory criteria for fair use and determined that fair use was not an appropriate defense in that situation. The court made two important points in its discussion which should be helpful to the educator and the librarian.

First, if the purpose of a use is commercial, then it would be presumed that the use is an unfair exploitation of another individual's copyrights. This should be distinguished with the position taken by the Court in the case of *Sony Corporation of America v. Universal Cities Studios*.[13] In *Sony*, the court determined that home taping of copyrighted television programs for personal use was protected under the concept of fair use. The Court stated that this noncommercial use shifted the burden to the copyright owner to prove the likelihood of future harm to the market value of the copyrighted work.

The second important point made by the Court in *Nation* was that the single most important element of fair use was the effect of the infringing copying on the market value of the copyrighted work.

Thus, one might assume that copying for educational purposes would fairly well insulate an individual from a claim of copyright infringment since it would be for a non-profit use, and probably not affect the market value of the copyrighted work. However, two cases indicate that this is not true. First, New York University was sued for copyright infringement because a number of faculty members had made multiple copies of copyrighted works and, in effect, created textual materials from these copyrighted works for use by their students.[14] New York University settled this case by agreeing to adopt the minimum standards for copying for classroom use as the maximum standards for such copying at NYU.[15] A more extreme example of what can happen to a faculty member who makes unauthorized copies of a copyrighted work, even if it is for classroom use, is detailed in the case of *Marcus v. Rowley*.[16] In *Marcus*, a school teacher had written and copyrighted a booklet on cake decorating. Another teacher copied part of the booklet in preparing her own booklet to give to her students. The original author filed a lawsuit claiming a copyright infringement by the other teacher. In this case the 9th Circuit looked to the conduct of the alleged infringer and noted that she did not try to obtain permission from and gave no credit to the author for the use of the materials. Although the Court of Appeals acknowledged the trial court's finding that the copying probably had no effect on the market for the booklet, the Court stated that the defense of fair use was not available in this case because "the mere absence of measurable pecuniary damage does not require the finding of fair use. . . . fair use is to be considered by a consideration of all the evidence in the case" (cit. omitted).[17] The Court then referenced the Publisher's Guidelines as a standard which would be helpful in determining what would constitute fair use.

Thus, since a faculty member and the librarian would run a substantial risk of having a copyright infringement action filed against them should multiple copying be done beyond that allowed under the Publisher's Guidelines, it is usually best to try to obtain permission from the copyright owner to make multiple copies of the work. While the most prudent action would be to obtain permission prior to making multiple copies, this may not be possible. Often it is a slow process to obtain permission, and it may be difficult, if not impossible, to obtain a royalty-free right to use the material. Since most colleges and universities are not in a position to charge students extra fees in order to pay copying costs for supplemental materials, the failure to obtain the right to reproduce journal articles without royalty payments may make such permission of limited utility.

A good example of the problems faced by a faculty member who may attempt to obtain permission to reproduce a number of copies of journal articles for classroom use was detailed in a 1986 article in the *Journal of College and University Law*. A faculty member determined in the fall of the year that an advanced science course which was to be taught in the following spring quarter, would require the use of over 90 articles, most of which were published in scholarly journals. Since the articles were selected well in advance of the course and multiple copies were to be made of a substantial amount of material, it is likely that the Publisher's Guidelines for fair use would not be met. As a result, the faculty member attempted to obtain permission by writing letters to 17 publishers. Two of the letters were returned to the faculty member. One was sent to the wrong publisher, and two publishers did not respond. An additional response was received after the course was over. Of the publishers who did respond, permission was given to make copies with no charge by nine publishers covering forty-nine articles. Eight of the publishers requested payment. The payments requested range from $.02 per page per student to $1.75 per page, with the average cost being $1.35 per page. Permission had been requested to make copies for 25 students. However, one publisher requested payment for making a minimum of 100 copies even though permission was requested to make only 25 copies. Another publisher charged 15 cents per page, per student for multiple copies of an article which was authored by the faculty member teaching the course. The faculty member decided not to make the multiple copies, because the cost would have been $108 per student for permission to use the articles, and an additional $25 per student to make the copies. This would have meant a total expenditure of over $3,000 for the one-time use of the articles in a course consisting of 25 students.[18]

In light of the experience described above, it is difficult to determine what course of action a librarian or a faculty member should take if journal articles are needed for classroom use. It would indeed be unfortunate if college and university students were unable to have reasonable access to important scholarly material simply because of the fear of copyright infringement. Since one of the purposes of the copyright law is to encourage the dissemination of ideas, this certainly cannot be a result desired by Congress. However, publishers would no doubt argue that they too have the right to have a reasonable return on their investment in scholarly publications. Also since the market for such publications is generally limited, it is important for them to control copying activities. Nevertheless, one would think that the in-class use of such articles would actually contribute to the eventual market for these journals by demonstrating the utility of the journal to the student.

Perhaps a better solution to any of the situations discussed above would be for the Copyright Clearance Center (CCC) to expand its activities so that any faculty member wishing to make multiple copies for classroom use could do so, at a reasonable cost, under a license obtained by his or her university. However, it is essential that the process used by the CCC be both simple and economical. Perhaps a good model for the CCC would be the site licenses developed by the American Society of Composers, Authors, and Performers (ASCAP) and Broadcast Music, Inc. (BMI) for the performance of music on college campuses.[19] The "one-tier license" available from these organizations allows institutions to perform publicly copyrighted materials in a wide range of musical activities. This license is issued to an institution in exchange for an annual fee which is based on the number of equivalent full-time students in attendance at that institution. These licenses have been effective and accepted by colleges and universities and the music industry because they are reasonably priced and simple to obtain. In order to promote the wide dissemination of scholarly materials in the classrooms of our nation's colleges and universities and also to provide some financial protection to authors and publishers, a reasonable licensing program which would allow multiple copying of copyrighted materials for classroom use must be developed.

REFERENCES

1. H.R. REP. NO. 1476, 94th Cong., 1st sess. 68-70 (1976) (Agreement on Guidelines for Classroom Copying in Not-For-Profit Educational Institutions).
2. *See generally, Marcus v. Rowely*, 695 F. 2d 1171 (9th Cir. 1983).
3. 17 U.S.C. Section 101, et. seq.
4. *See, Harper and Row Publishers, Inc. v. National Enterprises*, 105 S.Ct., 2218, at 2223 (1985).
5. 17 U.S.C. Section. 106.
6. The scope of this article is not intended to discuss all the defenses of a potential copyright infringer. However, it is useful to point out that public colleges and universities and their libraries may well have an additional defense to a claim of copyright infringement other than those limitations on exclusive use which will be discussed in this article. The 11th amendment to the United States Constitution gives immunity to states from suits brought against them in Federal Court, unless Congress, acting pursuant to the 14th Amendment has abrogated the 11th Amendment immunity to the states. There is currently an open question as to whether or not a state is immune to an action under the copyright law. At least one court in *Johnson v. University of Virginia*, 606 F. Supp. 321 (W.D.Va. 1985) determined that the 11th Amendment would not bar a damage award against the state. However, several other courts have held to the contrary. For example, in *Richard Anderson Photography v. Radford University*, 633 F. Supp. 1154 (W.D.Va. 1986) the court determined that 11th Amendment immunity is available for a state entity. Further, the 11th Circuit Court of Appeals in the case of *Cardinal Industries, Inc. v. Anderson Parrish Associates, Inc.* upheld the dismissal of the copyright infringement action against a state university employee on the grounds that the employee was afforded protection by the 11th Amendment. The Supreme Court of the United State refused to grant ceritiorari in this action (See, 56 U.S.L.W. 3243 [1987]). Thus the breadth and scope of the 11th Amendment immunity in a copyright action is unsettled.
7. 17 U.S.C. Section 108.
8. 17 U.S.C. Section 108.
9. Report of the Register of Copyrights: Library Reproduction of Copyrighted Works (17 U.S.C. 108) (January, 1983) and *Impact of the Copyright Law in College Teaching*, Gail Paulus Sorenson, 12 Journal of College and University Law, 509, 521-522 (1986).
10. 17 U.S.C. Section 108 (b) & (c).
11. 17 U.S.C. Section 107.
12. 105 S. Ct. 2218 (1985).
13. 464 U.S. 417 (1984).
14. *See, Addison-Wesley Publishing Co. v. New York University*, No. 82 Civ. 8333 (S.D.N.Y.) April 7, 1983.
15. Ibid.
16. 695 Fed. 2d. 1171 (9th Cir. 1983).

17. Ibid., at 1177.

18. *Impact of the Copyright Law on College Teaching*, Gail Paulus Sorenson, 12 Journal of College and University Law, 509, 515-518 (1986).

19. See ASCAP, Colleges and Universities Experimental License Agreement, One Lincoln Plaza, New York, NY 10023; and BMI, 320 West 57th Street, New York, NY 10019.

Accessing Electronic Journals: A Survey of Canadian and American Libraries

Ann Okerson

Many of the papers presented at gatherings such as this deal with automating the processes associated with periodicals. In working on this project, my colleagues and I were concerned with automation of the periodicals themselves. This paper briefly presents the results of a survey of current use of electronic technologies in accessing periodical literature and discusses the implications of the findings as well as some of the theoretical and practical considerations involved. Because of the limitations of our time here, I will present a shortened version of the responses, but if any of you are interested in more detail, please leave your name and we will send you more complete information.

Doing a survey in an area where products and technologies are changing is an interesting and elusive process. Printed information may be unavailable or outdated, and one of the best means of finding out what is going on is to telephone and ask "what are you doing this month?" Before I begin, then, I would like to acknowledge some particularly helpful sources. They are Linda Futato, Marketing Director at Federal Document Retrieval in Washington, D.C., retrieval specialists and publishers of *Directory of Periodicals Online*. Another individual who steered me in right directions was John Paul Ehmard at Meckler Corporation and editor of *CD-ROMs in Print*. John Tagler of Elsevier gave me several hours and Christopher Pooley of SilverPlatter, the largest producer of CD-

---

Ann Okerson, Manager, Library Services, Jerry Alper Inc., 271 Main Street, P.O. Box 218, Eastchester, NY 10707.

ROM library products, was accidentally captive in the seat next to mine going to ALA Midwinter.

The survey was conducted by Hana Komorous and Elena Romaniuk, Serials Librarians at the University of Victoria in British Columbia, and me. They sent out questionnaires to 84 Canadian libraries in institutions defined as "universities." I sent letters and questionnaires to 99 ARL libraries in the United States. Our goals were to learn about current library practice in accessing periodicals electronically and to see if such practice was displacing standard access via printed subscriptions. In pooling our results, from two different countries and from what turned out to be greatly dissimilar academic libraries, we ended up with some apple/orange problems, as you will see.

For purposes of our survey, the definition of an electronic periodical was: "A full-text electronic periodical is a serial publication in machine-readable form, delivered via computer to the user directly (as on CD-ROM), or over a telecommunications network, but not necessarily only available in electronic format." Or to state it another way, the library can (1) access from a remote database, such as ISI or Chemical Abstracts or Harvard Business Review, either by direct connection or through a service such as DIALOG or BRS, or (2) hold the material in the library on a 5.25 inch iridescent compact disk which is read by a laser beam via computer interface. However, the availability of periodicals online is far more extensive than on CD-ROM, which is so recent a technology that the range of products is very limited. Also, there has been very little periodical material created specifically for either technology. What is available tends to be a simultaneous version or by-product of information produced in paper form.

There may be other electronic technologies in the development stages which may or may not affect daily library life: different types of optical disks, optical cards, or digital tapes, but they are not considered in this survey.

Let us review briefly the differences between access online and via CD-ROM. Online being stored offsite, the library neither mounts, updates, nor owns the information in any way. It simply accesses the files and pays for the online connect time as well as for access to the particular files or records. Simply speaking, all that is needed at the library end is someone who knows how to locate and search the appropriate files, a computer, a modem, and money to pay the bill for the searching/access. In real life, the searching often requires skills and the charges for any but a quick search can be very costly. At the same time, online searching is much more rapid and comprehensive than a paper search in the equivalent amount of time, as one can quickly deal with a variety of authors, titles, subjects, keywords, or whatever one needs to check. Costs rise in proportion to the amount of information sought. Therefore, costs are elusive and unpredictable, while library budgets are fixed.

With CD-ROM, the costs are known as the outset: (1) purchase of the necessary computer, drive, and software to search and run the ROM disk, as well as printer, work area, and other physical requirements which need to be met. The cost of such a workstation has been estimated at as much as $8,000.[1] (2) The cost of the subscription, which varies according to the product, from several hundred dollars to perhaps $20,000 per year. There may also be an annual licensing fee for retaining and using old disks. Once these upfront charges are accounted for, search time is virtually free and the investment is maximized by encouraging use of the workstation and the CD-ROM product around the clock.

Because CD-ROM is searched electronically, it mimics online searching in its rapidity and flexibility. Furthermore, user-friendly software makes it easy for the end-user to do the search without the intervention of an information specialist. Library experience suggests that CD-ROM use by patrons is enthusiastic and lineups are common.

CD-ROM technology has had its drawbacks. It is new and lack of standardization of the hardware, software, and disks themselves have posed problems. However, in recent months these problems seem well under way to resolution, so that libraries can be fairly certain of using workstations for more than one product. The next problem being worked on is that of having multiple access points to CD-ROM databases, instead of having one workstation for one specific database usable by one person at a time as is presently the case. Once that is resolved, we are told it will be feasible to add remote access to the systems so that patrons can dial up these databases. At least the beginnings of all this is promised us by the end of 1988.

If you are asking why we surveyed only academic libraries and didn't canvas special or public or other libraries, we recognized that there are simply too many of these institutions and we thought, therefore, that we should stay with institutions we know best. Turning to the questionnaire, we asked the following questions:

ONLINE:

1. Does your library provide online searching services?
2. What types of databases are searched? Bibliographic? Full text? Numeric/factual? Other?
3. When you search full text databases, do you search newspapers, newsletters, journals, reference works, books, reports, government publications, other? This was done as a checklist and we asked for examples.
4. When accessing full text electronic periodicals, what areas do you cover? We provided another 7-part checklist and further subdivided sciences disciplines into 10 subjects.

CD-ROM:

5. Do you search any full text databases locally on CD-ROM? Which ones? Do any include periodicals?

OTHER:

6. Who are your users?
7. Do you provide services and facilities to allow your users to do their own searching?
8. If you are not currently searching full text databases, do you have plans to do so?

Ample space was provided throughout for comments as to when and how periodical access and full text searching were employed. Of the 106 libraries that responded 64 (of 84) were Canadian and 42 (of 99) were U.S. In a survey this size, the statistical variation expected is approximately 10%, so that should be kept in mind. Certainly one learns that Canadian libraries are more willing to respond to questionnaires than U.S. libraries. One suspects this is because U.S. libraries, particularly ARL libraries, are constantly surveyed and protect themselves against surveys which are absolutely required.

Here are the findings that seem of significance:

1. There was a mixed population of respondents: directors, assistant directors, reference librarians or heads of reference, collection development librarians, individual subject specialists, and (1/3 of the time in U.S. libraries) a "searching co-ordinator." Once again, we see that while academic libraries perform similar functions, organizational patterns vary.
2. Seven percent of respondents did no electronic searching at all. (Only 1 U.S. library did no electronic searching at all.) Seventy-three percent did at least bibliographic and full text database searching, but 21% specifically commented they did full text searching rarely, leaving 52% who did not quantify in any way.
3. U.S. libraries were 2.5 times more likely to do a variety of online searching, including full text, than Canadian libraries. (The reasons for this might be that ARL libraries are richer than the Canadian institutions surveyed; that there is a differential of approximately 25% in the exchange rate; that there are far more U.S. databases.) This difference could be a window on differences between U.S. libraries and those of other Western countries. Doing some preliminary correlating between size of library and amount of electronic accessing, we feel that institutional philosophy rather than budget size was the overriding factor in amount of electronic use.
4. The greatest use of full text online was newspapers (68%) next came journals (60%); and reference books (35%). Uses of other types of material were significantly lower. There was no enormous variation between U.S. and Canadian libraries, except that American libraries were 5 times more likely to access newsletters online and had about 30% higher use of government publications.
5. Under full text use of periodicals/journals, the major uses were:

news media (magazines, letters, services):	57%
sciences:	40%
business:	40%
law:	23%

6. Within the above breakdown, the largest amount of full text periodical use was the hard sciences in the U.S., closely followed by health/medicine. In Canada, health/medicine dominates online use, with hard sciences far behind.
7. Moving to CD-ROM use, in Canada it is hardly a factor at all. Only 4 out of 64 libraries said they searched any full text on CD-ROM. About 1/3 of U.S. libraries search full text on CD-ROM. Most of that searching was done on *Disclosure*, the business database.
8. Do you allow end-user searches? Only 12 of the responding Canadian libraries do; over half the responding U.S. libraries do. More specifically, 10 of 42 U.S. libraries allow users access to inexpensive systems, mostly BRS After Dark; and 20 of the 42 give users access to CD-ROM. So, answering "yes" to end-user searching meant, in general, that libraries allow their users to access CD-ROM databases but not do online searching as such.

As with all surveys, inexperienced surveyors think of a number of questions that were implicit but should have been explicitly asked to achieve desired information. For example: How often do you search online? How many hours a week? What is the budget? How has that changed? What are specific future plans?

Moving to written comments we received, the most frequent ones were:

1. There really isn't a lot of demand by our users for full text searching.
2. Online searching, let alone full text, is very expensive and we can't afford much of it. Maybe when it's cheaper.
3. We are not given to jumping on technological bandwagons.
4. We have terrific paper collections, so we use those.
5. The journals and newspapers that are available online are core titles to which we would have to subscribe anyhow. It would

be much more helpful to have esoteric titles; that would represent a savings for the library. I found that comment surprising, as the latest edition of *Directory of Periodicals Online* lists 7,742 periodicals available full text, partially, or abstracted in Volume 1 (Business, Law, and News) alone.
6. We are planning to enter into or expand all the above areas as time and money permit.

Several conclusions were apparent:

1. Users of online services often do not know what is "out there." This is not surprising, because it changes constantly. Cuadra Associates say in their introduction to *Directory of Online Databases* that whereas there were about 400 online databases at the beginning of the decade, there were about 3,500 at the end of 1987.[2] Unless the library has money to hire or invest in training very knowledgeable staff, it will always run behind developments. Some of the lack of demand perceived above may well be due to lack of knowledge and marketing on the library's part.
2. Despite excitement among enthusiasts and lots of discussion in library literature, online searching is accepted in a very limited way by academic libraries, the search of indexes for bibliographic citations now almost old hat.
3. There is confusion about definitions. Respondents do make a distinction between newspapers and periodicals but probably do not make a distinction between periodicals and indexing/abstracting services. That is, ERIC and NTIS were listed by some as examples of full text searching. This probably means that is much less use of full-text periodical searching than the 52% survey results indicate.
4. There is confusion about what full-text searching really IS as well as its proper role in the library. Were respondents thinking about simply locating full text articles and retrieving them or were they talking about SEARCHING full text, a quite different concept. Also when would one do any or either of those?
5. The future is not clear. CD-ROM is an upstart technology first actively demonstrated at Midwinter in 1985, which may

change library behavior with respect to online searching. So far, there is really very little available on CD-ROM. *Guide to CD-ROMs in Print*, first edition, summer 1987, identified about 100 products. The 2nd edition, due for ALA in July 1988, will identify about 300.[3] Of these, about 40% are library oriented products.[4] At present, it is estimated that libraries own 10,000 CD-COM units, to reach about one million by the end of 1991,[5] but that at least half of these are for internal bibliographic use, such as cataloguing and catalogue access.
6. There was no indication that libraries are, at this time, replacing current paper holdings with remote access to equivalent materials online.

What does all this have to do with NASIG members attending the 3rd annual conference? For those who work in the information industry or in corporate or medical or special libraries where searching and retrieval is as common as chickens laying eggs, you may use this 20 minutes to feel complacent. You have come to the future, have mastered it, and are qualified to speak at future conferences. For those who work in more traditional libraries, you may feel that once again the status quo has been confirmed. You may say that some surveyors went in search of the Brave New World and once again established that while 1984 arrived chronologically, philosophically it won't come to pass until after your retirement date.

Gee-whizzery for its own sake is always fun, but it needs a context to make an impact, and that context is now arriving. Several significant changes have taken place even since 1984. While librarians are not considered innovators, they do eventually respond to change and innovation. What has changed?

1. Computers and high-tech communications are increasingly taken for granted. Many of us who did not work with automation 5 years ago or did not have computers near our desks, probably do now. Even the tortoises among us, and I include myself here, have either bought or are thinking of owning a home or desk computer. Not only are our children computer literate, but we are learning as well. Prices continue to drop. Ownership breeds familiarity. So it's not scary to deal with

microchips anymore. Once we own hardware and software, we want to maximize its use. We even like it. Some of us become obsessed.
2. The pricing direction of computers and communications, still downward, is in direct contrast to the trends in pricing of library materials. We are all intensely aware of the problem that high periodical prices have become. Libraries of all sizes are coping by cancelling duplicate and "fringy" titles, sacrificing monographs, cutting back on binding, and mounting educational programs with faculties and administrations to get dollars or at least sympathy. It's my own belief that many libraries are doing so hoping that economic prosperity, a stronger dollar, or a more powerful argument vis-à-vis other elements on campus will restore buying power enabling them to once again collect most of what they want within their own four walls. This is hardly a viable collection development philosophy in our age, where political conservatism and world economics have a local effect which no one would have predicted. Global interconnectivity causes the pendulum to take ever broader and more temporary swings.
3. There is a real explosion of knowledge and information, as well as publication, and it is difficult to make the judgment, as some librarians and scholars suggest, that an increasing proportion of it is unnecessary, self-aggrandizing hackwork. In fact, it is difficult to make accurate judgments about new, highly interdisciplinary, rapidly evolving fields, let alone all the familiar ones we know and love. There is more and more material to choose from. There is certainly an explosion of technology and the smorgasbord becomes a richer, more varied one.
4. In the past few years, more libraries are undergoing or have undergone retrospective conversion projects, and knowledge of library holdings can be much more broadly shared among institutions. OCLC and RLIN databases have grown larger and are powerful tools for identification of library resources.

All those things being true, we haven't the promise of a rose garden but of an unmade bed and years of ambiguity. The only thing most of our institutions can afford to do, and it's finance and not leadership that takes us there, is to let go of a lot of what we have historically expected to be able to hold unto ourselves. We must come to think of our library as a flexible organism and other libraries, electronic databanks, document delivery services as our remote storage locations. Instead of being collection and size-oriented, we will increasingly become patron- and use-oriented.

There are large problems with judging a library by quality of service and breadth of access, because we haven't developed good standards to do that, but we will. There are large problems with amending traditional notions of acquisitions and reference work, because staff become anxious about jobs, but if those of us who graduated in the '60s and '70s can't readjust and rethink, the newer librarians enthusiastically will.

The idea of the flexible, user-driven library is, however, a freeing one in ways we haven't fully appreciated yet. We stop worrying so much about what happens if we fail to buy precisely the right books; a subscription we can't place doesn't cause sleepless nights, nor does an unreceived issue or a periodical out for binding. Mistakes are not irreparable. The needed article in the latest issue of *Brain Research* that hasn't been checked in yet (though the faculty member saw a colleague's copy last week) can be ordered quickly.

If someone is standing at NASIG #8 talking to you of such matters, I expect they will tell you that substantial portions of the acquisitions budgets are going toward document delivery services, online retrieval, CD-ROM, possibly optical cards, and local area networks which make it possible for more users to access more electronic information more easily. There will be discussion of tradeoffs in pricing, as the same products are available from publishers in several different and viable formats: paper, online, optical disk, selectively, or maybe even custom packaged journals created specifically to our own profile requirements. Existing publishers will be struggling with having products in one form compete with the same product in another form and with document delivery services also supplying their products. Who should charge, whom should be charged and how much?

One hopes that talking about over-priced library subscriptions will have expanded into a larger concern about what we are paying for all types of materials and whether our buying philosophies are right for our own institutional needs. Maybe we will even be thinking about how we want materials published and packaged for us, instead of reacting to what publishers provide.

What do we do for now? Those who work in processing areas, get out and ask to use some new products and technologies. Try INFOTRAC or DISCLOSURE or ERIC on CD-ROM. Ask for an introduction to online searching. Try to do your own search on serial pricing or retrieval or your favorite hobby. Imagine yourself dealing not with 200 new subscriptions per year but 1,000 articles as part of your regular job. Should the reference librarians be providing that acquisition service? Should technical services become a visible public service? Listen to all the new ideas with skepticism but muster some enthusiasm because it isn't going away and it's kind of different and kind of fun. It IS liberating to think about a different kind of library of the future and a different job, not just this same one for years.

With this sort of freedom of the imagination comes serious responsibility not to lose heart, not to lose energy, and most important, in an age when it suddenly seems possible to promise anything, not to promise more than we can realistically deliver.

Philip Roth said, when addressing a group of people recently (and perhaps I'm remembering his words incorrectly) that it is his experience that most such honors inevitably go to the wrong people. That being the case, I'm probably the wrong person to talk to you on such matters, but they are some of the most interesting matters around.

REFERENCES

1. "Electronic technology and serials publishing," *Library Systems Newsletter*, 6(11), November 1986, p. 83.
2. "Preface," *Directory of Online Databases*, 8(3), 1988, p.v.
3. John Paul Ehmard in telephone conversation 5/9/88.
4. Collier, Harry, "Where is CD-ROM? Some brief product reviews," *Electronic and Optical Publishing Review*, 7(2), June 1987, p.72.
5. Sieck, Steven, "CO-ROM industry review and outlook," New York, Link Resources Marketing, 1988 (report in progress).

ADONIS
and Electronically Stored Information:
An Information Broker's Experience

Constance Orchard

BACKGROUND

The ADONIS project is a trial document delivery service which supplies full-text, laser-printed copies of articles appearing in 219 current biomedical journals which are stored on CD-ROM. The ADONIS project was formally conceived in 1980 after Elsevier Science Publishers and the then British Library Lending Division (BLLD) undertook a major survey to determine what articles were being requested and in what volume. All of the requests received at the BLLD during a two-week period were analyzed. It was determined that biomedical articles, less than 3-1/2 years old, were most frequently requested. Approximately 50% of the articles demanded appeared in issues less than 3-1/2 years old, and approximately 60% were from biomedical titles. Two subsequent document delivery surveys have since confirmed these results. (It is interesting to note that the original survey was one of the earliest examples of commercial and non-commercial organizations undertaking joint research in the area of scientific communication.)

Once the most frequently requested and photocopied scientific, technical and medical (STM) journals had been identified, a consortium of publishers, libraries and document supply centers began investigating other economically viable ways to disseminate these materials. During the years 1980-1983 technical and financial consultants determined that, although technologically possible, electronic information storage was not an economically viable alterna-

---

Constance Orchard, Director of Marketing, Information on Demand, Inc., 2020 Milvia Street, Berkeley, CA 94704.

© 1988 by The Haworth Press, Inc. All rights reserved.

tive to traditional labor intensive methods of document delivery. A single workstation necessary for retrieval had an estimated cost of $250,000.00.

It is worth noting here that because of the strong competition between non-commercial, subsidized, and commercial, non-subsidized document supply centers, the pricing of all documents was, and still is, well below real costs. The delivery of articles retrieved from the ADONIS disks is also subject to these same financial considerations. Consequently, in 1983, ADONIS was an economically prohibitive venture for commercial document suppliers.

In 1985 technological advances led to the development of CD-ROM and relatively inexpensive laser printers. CD-ROM proved to be a much better storage medium than the earlier 12-inch disks. It allowed for the storage of larger amounts of information at significantly reduced costs. In addition the costs of the retrieval workstation had decreased considerably to their present price of $25,000.00.

Having overcome concerns about economic feasibility, the ADONIS group was able to acquire support from several major European libraries and the Commission of European Communities. At the same time, an agreement between the European, the U.S. and the Japanese Patent Offices to create an optical store of all patent documents allowed the ADONIS group to employ the services of an already existing scanning facility in Europe.

In 1986 the ADONIS publishers agreed to conduct a trial program, the ADONIS Project, which would demonstrate that publishers could recoup losses from their declining subscription bases and extensive photocopying without adding to the financial burden of the library community. The plan was that the ADONIS publishers would supply their journals to document delivery centers in machine-readable form for the printing of individual articles on demand. The main objectives were:

— to learn about the impact of such a service on document delivery in general;
— to explore applications of optical/digital technology;
— to examine the economics of supplying individual STM articles.

TECHNICAL DETAILS

Each week, the contents of 219 biomedical journals published by the ADONIS group of publishers, after January 1987, are indexed by bibliographic detail at Excerpta Medica in Amsterdam. A unique ADONIS number is assigned to each article, and the full text of the material, along with its ASCII index, is sent to the scanning facility. The scanning is performed in two modes—"threshold" and "dither." "Threshold" is used for text scanning, and essentially reduces each area on a page to either black or white. "Dither" mode is used to scan halftones and other graphics which require gradation. Although the threshold method of scanning uses much less storage space than the dither method of scanning, the publishers decided to employ both methods because of the need for extremely detailed reproductions which the large percentage of graphics and halftones in biomedical materials (approximately 20%) necessitates.

Today, pages containing only textual material are scanned in the threshold mode. Using the threshold mode image retrieval is very fast and document print quality is very high. Pages containing both text and graphics or halftones, however, require scanning in the dither mode. In this instance image retrieval is slower due to the increased disk storage space required, but the print quality of the graphics and halftones is very high. The print quality of the text, however, does vary somewhat.

Although technologically impossible today, in the future one page containing text and graphics or halftones will be scanned by both the threshold and dither modes producing a high quality of both text and graphics or halftones.

Once the scanning is complete, a master disk is produced by Philips and Du Pont Optical Company in Hannover, West Germany, and copy disks are sent to the participating document supply centers around the world.

The ADONIS workstation, developed by the British Library in conjunction with the Commission of the European Communities, consists of a Laser Data System with an IBM PC, an Hitachi CD-

ROM drive and a Ricoh laser printer. The software maintains a log of articles copied and provides the basis for the calculation of royalties.

The original partners in the consortium, Blackwell Scientific Publications Ltd., Elsevier Science Publishers, Pergamon Journals, Ltd. and Springer-Verlag GmbH have since been joined by six other publishers: Butterworth Scientific Ltd., Churchill Livingstone, the C.V. Mosby Company, Munksgaard International Publishers Ltd., Georg Thieme Verlag, and John Wiley & Sons Ltd. It is these publishers and the document delivery centers who are sharing the costs of this 2-1/2 year trial period.

The worldwide participating document distribution centers include: the British Library Document Supply Centre, Boston Spa; CDST Paris; ICYT, Madrid; Karolinska Institute, Stockholm; KNAW, Amsterdam; Medical Library, Cologne; Information on Demand, Berkeley; University Microfilms, Ann Arbor; University of Monterray, Mexico; National Library of Australia, Canberra; and Kinokuniya, Japan.

THE ADONIS COLLECTION

Through extensive discussions with the participating document distribution centers it was determined that in the absence of a disk jukebox, it would be impractical to manually work with a collection of materials that included more information than could be contained on one disk per week. The ADONIS group, therefore, had to balance the storage limitations of one 550MB CD-ROM with the need to include an adequate number of journals in order to make the trial valid. One CD-ROM 550MB disk has the storage capacity of approximately 5,000 journal pages. Therefore, a collection confined to storage on 52 550MB CD-ROM disks per year (1 disk per week) has the storage capacity of 260,000 journal pages. Having determined this, the ADONIS group of publishers selected 219 core biomedical journals which would produce an estimated 57 disks per year, for the trial.

Some representative titles include: *American Heart Journal*; *Archives of Toxicology*; *Brain Research*; *Cellular and Molecular Biol-*

ogy; *Computers in Biology and Medicine*; *The Journal of Molecular and Cellular Immunology*; *Leukemia Research*; and *Toxicology*.

IOD'S EXPERIENCE WITH THE ADONIS PROJECT

Hardware and Software

As with any trial project, there have been delays and malfunctions associated with the ADONIS project. Some of the problems experienced at IOD included: faulty laser data monitor boards which had to be replaced three times; code errors in early versions of the software which made some disks unreadable; relatively slow search and print time. However, most problems have been resolved and further enhancements are being identified. For example, upcoming versions of the software promise to list the issues that are represented on any particular CD-ROM in the ADONIS collection, and the field lengths of the users' address information will be expanded.

The possibility of producing ADONIS disks using Digital Video Interactive (DVI) is being pursued. DVI, a new technology introduced by General Electric, allows for compression ratios of 120:1 and a ten times faster disk access speed. One DVI ADONIS disk would be able to store 60,000 to 65,000 journal pages, thereby increasing storage capacity of a disk ten fold.

ADONIS Order Volume

IOD began to offer its clients document retrieval from the ADONIS collection of titles dated January 1987 to the present in November 1987. In an effort to determine what the existing demand is for the ADONIS service IOD has tracked: the number of biomedical orders received; the number of orders fulfilled through the ADONIS collection of journals; the number of orders received for ADONIS titles published prior to 1987.

In the period from November 1987 through April 1988, 5% of all biomedical document orders received by IOD have been orders for documents contained in the ADONIS collection. During that same period approximately four times as many more requests were received for titles published prior to 1987 than were received for material which is included in the ADONIS collection.

Since February 1988, IOD has seen a substantial increase in the volume of orders received for ADONIS journal documents. However, this volume is still extremely low when compared to the number of orders for non-ADONIS biomedical documents.

Several factors account for the relatively low demand for ADONIS titles:

a. The 219 journals contained in the ADONIS collection represent only approximately 5% of the total biomedical literature collection of about 4,000 publications. Interestingly, this 5% coincides precisely with the percentage of ADONIS title orders IOD receives.
b. The continuing lack of awareness, within the U.S. library community, about the ADONIS CD-ROM collection contributes to the low volume of orders received. As IOD's efforts to educate potential users about the availability of ADONIS titles continues, the order volume should increase.
c. References to STM articles do not appear until several months after their publication. As more references to the 1987-1988 ADONIS titles begin to appear in the biomedical literature and electronic databases, the demand for those titles will increase.

The advent of new technology such as DVI, or a CD-ROM jukebox, will certainly allow for increased journal coverage and consequently increased demand for ADONIS titles.

THE FUTURE OF CD-ROM PUBLISHING

As stated earlier, the main objectives of the ADONIS project are to learn about the impact of such a service on document delivery, to explore applications of optical/digital technology and to examine the economics of supplying individual STM articles.

At this point in time, it is extremely difficult, if not impossible, to draw any conclusions about the impact optical/digital technology may have on document delivery and publishing from the ADONIS project. Until such time that a significant proportion of biomedical publications are added to the ADONIS collection, particularly key journals such as *The New England Journal of Medicine*, *Journal of the American Medical Association* and *Lancet*, a concrete evaluation of the potential impact of CD-ROM publishing will continue to be elusive. However, there is a very strong indication that CD-ROM publishing will have an enormous impact on the publishing industry. At a time when there is an increasing market for the supply of individual articles as well as an increasing number of publications, libraries, having limited budgets and limited storage space, are being forced to choose carefully the publications to which they subscribe.

As the spread of personal workstations and the development of computer networks continues, optical/digital technology, providing both convenience in terms of storage, accessibility and reproductive quality, will become increasingly important. CD-ROM theoretically could remove altogether the need for print on paper journals.

Serial Article Identifiers—
SISAC, BIBLID, NISO, ISO, ANSI and ADONIS:
A Confusion of Alphabet Soup

Sandra K. Paul

Two different methods have been developed for identifying the articles in serial publications. To further complicate the matter, these two methods are known by three different acronyms and are the product of four different organizations, SISAC, NISO, ISO, ADONIS.

The Serial Issue and Article Identifier (SAID) was developed by a group of librarians, publishers, subscription agents and technical specialists functioning simultaneously under the sponsorship of the Serials Industry Systems Advisory Committee (SISAC) and the National Information Standards Organization (NISO). The SAID is composed of the same data elements as BIBLID, the serial issue identifier developed by the International Organization for Standardization (ISO). Supported by European and American journal publishers, the ADONIS Identifier was developed by the ADONIS document delivery system. (See Figure 1.)

This talk will cover the history of these two systems for identifying serial articles and the organizations which developed them. It describes: the purposes each identifier is intended to serve; the functions it supports; and the uses to which it might be put by NASIG members and their constituents.

Sandra K. Paul, SKP Associates, 160 Fifth Avenue, New York, NY 10010.

This paper was presented at the conference by Minna C. Saxe, Chief Serials Librarian, Graduate School Library, City University of New York and ALA Representative to SISAC and Vice Chair of SISAC.

© 1988 by The Haworth Press, Inc. All rights reserved.

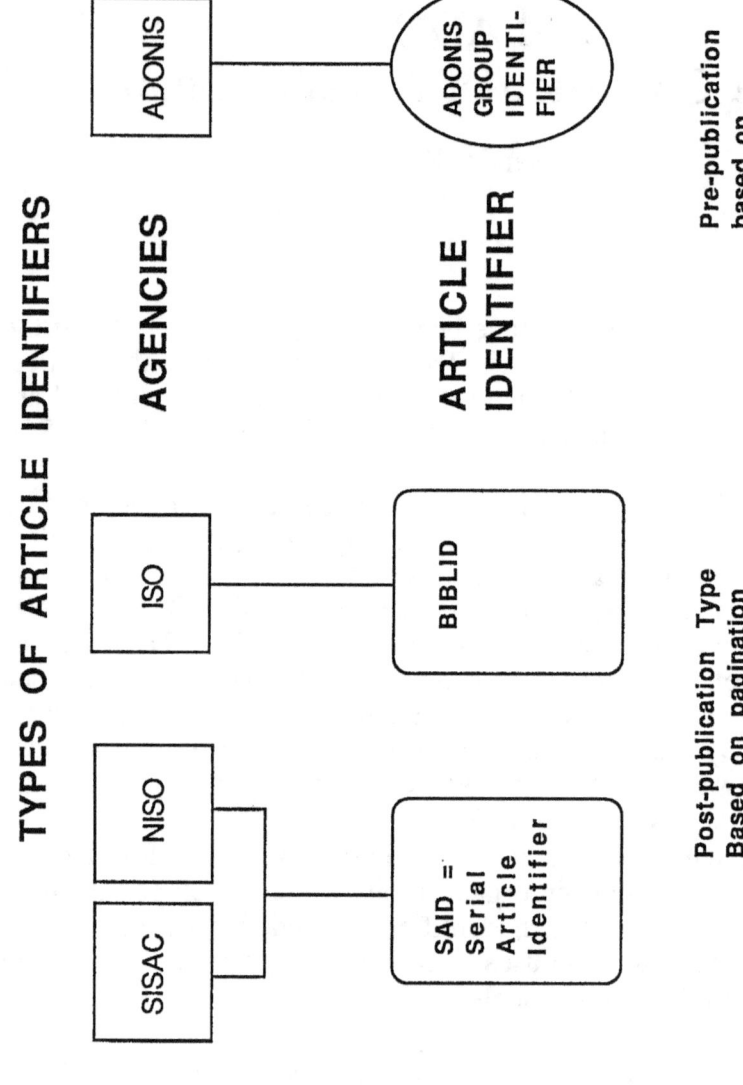

FIGURE 1

HISTORY AND IDENTIFIER CONTENT

SISAC was formed in 1982 by the Book Industry Study Group, Inc. Under the direction of its first Chairperson, Richard Rowe of The Faxon Company, Inc., SISAC hoped to develop:

— A unique identifier for each issue of each serial publication;
— A unique identifier for each article in a given serial issue;
— A bar code in which these identifiers would appear;
— A set of computer-to-computer formats to allow for the electronic ordering and claiming of serial publications.

Having achieved these initial aims, SISAC, now chaired by Mary E. Curtis of Transaction, is taking these advantages, and is extending them to the publishing community. In addition, SISAC is planning to undertake the development of a computer-to-computer format for serial invoicing, and to develop other formats and standards needed to support the library, vendor and publisher in an automated environment.

SAID *issue* identification incorporates information supplied by a publisher onto a given issue of a scientific, technical or scholarly serial publication. This information includes the: International Standard Serial Number (ISSN); date of publication; and volume, issue, part or whatever enumeration is printed on the periodical itself. The format for recording this information was developed by a SISAC subcommittee which had initially agreed that they were developing a format which should become an American National (ANSI) standard. They requested and received permission to function as a NISO Standards Committee. The identifier which was developed was deliberately designed to complement a comparable format under development within ISO Technical Committee 46. The ISO standard was approved and subsequently published as ISO 9115 "Documentation—Bibliographic Identification (BIBLID) of contributions in serials and books." At the same time the SAID was in the process of becoming an ANSI standard.

The serial *article* identifier selected by SAID developers uses only information that is currently available in citations to serial articles. As in BIBLID, when only one article starts on a given page, the number of the first page of the article is added to the issue identifier. If more than one article starts on a page, a string of letters representing the first letters of the words in the title of the article follows the page number.

ADONIS, a document delivery service conceived by European publishers, was intended to be used on the European communication network known as EURONET DIANNE. Although it has been in existence for seven years, ADONIS actually began converting journal articles onto CD-ROM and printing out copies upon request in 1987. Its article identifier is composed of an ISSN, the last two digits of the year of publication, and a publisher-assigned sequential article number. This sequential number, however, is currently assigned by ADONIS project management. (Based upon experiences in its test phase, ADONIS may ask publishers to assign identification numbers to "Letters to the Editors" and other serial issue content not normally thought of as an "article.")

USES FOR THE IDENTIFIERS

The SAID was developed for use in computer-to-computer ordering and claiming formats. It currently appears in the draft ANSI standard for that purpose. However, it was also envisioned as a code that could be used to replace the Copyright Clearance Center number for those who maintain records of photocopies by article or page number. Further, the SAID was considered to be an exciting, potential tool for document delivery systems, because it could be created by a computer from the basic elements shown in machine-readable files and databases.

Publishers have discussed the possibility of scanning the issue level identifier on serial publication covers and then scanning the article level add-on on either the table of contents or the first page of the article for document ordering and/or photocopy tracking. As the publishing, vendor and library communities learn more about this code, we are sure that a number of other uses will be identified: article tracking through the scanning of the issue level component at receiving stations; inventory taking; and single copy order picking and verification.

The ADONIS Identifier is currently used by U.S. and foreign ADONIS centers for document delivery requests which are based on queries of machine-readable, as well as hard copy references to serial articles. Currently the identifier is created by ADONIS staff from printed serial publications. It is intended, however, that the identifier be assigned as soon as an article has been approved and is being typeset. This will allow ADONIS to send the identifier, along with other basic information about forthcoming articles, to libraries and professionals in science and technology as a part of an "Alert Service" for the pre-publication ordering of articles. Delivery of the copies requested in these orders, as is currently the case, will be made from the CD-ROM copies of the printed page and thus assure the quality required for reproduction of charts, tables, photographs and illustrations.

Since the specific issue number of a publication and page number within that issue are unknown at the time the ADONIS number is needed for this Alert Service, the ADONIS Identifier *must* be independent of issue-specific information. Since the SAID *requires* issue-specific identification data, it cannot replace the ADONIS number for the purpose of pre-publication ordering of articles. However, once an article is published and cited, a new data element, the sequential number component of the ADONIS Identifier, must be added to the bibliographic citation if that number is to be used for retrieval. Consequently, SISAC believes that the ability of librarians to create the SAID, by computer, from the existing bibliographic data, mitigates against the success of using the ADONIS number for post-publication document delivery requests.

WHAT THE FUTURE HOLDS

On October 2, 1987 a meeting, chaired by David Russon of the BLDSC, was held at the British Library Document Supply Centre (BLDSC) at Boston Spa (England). Attendees included: Barrie Stern of ADONIS; Sandra K. Paul and Mary Ellen Clapper, representing SISAC; Jamie Cameron and Gillian Page, representing the Scientific Technical and Medical Publishers Journal Committee; and individuals from the University of Bradford (England) and the British Library.

The results of our in-depth discussion of the SAID, the ADONIS

Identifier, and the University of Bradford's "DOCMATCH" system for searching databases, resulted in the following conclusions:

- The SAID is much longer and more difficult to create manually than the ADONIS Identifier. However, it is equally unique and built upon an international standard method of identification of serial publications, issues and articles.
- The ADONIS Identifier cannot be replaced by the SAID if it is to function in an "Alert Service" which is distributed before the issue and page number of a printed article are known.
- In the future, it is anticipated that requests for copies sent to ADONIS by electronic systems and based on information in machine-readable databases, will carry the SAID, rather than ADONIS Identifier, as the numeric identifier of the article sought.
- Since the search software used in the ADONIS system can locate articles based on the bibliographic data elements in the SAID, there is no reason that both identification systems cannot co-exist, each serving the scholar, scientist and librarian at different times in the life of an article.

Quoting from the minutes of that meeting, "As a result of the meeting, the group agreed that it would be useful for members and other interested parties to prepare a document for a wider audience to draw attention to progress in this area and to encourage practical use."

The SISAC office will gladly share drafts of this document with interested NASIG members, and have assured the meeting participants that the final document will be publicized throughout the U.S. by SISAC.

Any NASIG member wanting more detailed information about the meeting or about SISAC should contact the author of this paper at: SISAC, 160 Fifth Avenue, New York, NY 10010; Telephone: 212-929-1393, Fax: 212-989-7542.

The Challenge of Cataloging Computer Files

Anna M. Wang

Are conventional paper and microformat serials going to disappear? Two articles, appropriately titled "New Look of Magazines"[1] and "CD-ROMs: The Laser's Edge in Data Storage"[2] exemplify the blooming of electronic serials in 1987. The intention of this paper is to inspire additional questions rather than to provide answers as to how the bibliographic control of serial microcomputer files should be accomplished.

As of December 29, 1987, there were only 116 serial bibliographic level records among the total of 16,578 machine-readable data file (MRDF) records in the cataloging subsystem of the OCLC database. Are libraries not cataloging serial computer files or are they waiting for the Library of Congress to distribute their MRDF records through tapes to OCLC? Several factors seem to be responsible for this situation. Some libraries do not have the resources to catalog computer files. They find them too costly to catalog just as in the 1970s microforms were considered too costly to catalog. In fact, it is more costly to maintain the bibliographic record. Additional equipment configurations for electronic publishing are constantly under development and cataloging rules and bibliographic input standards are constantly evolving. In short it is expensive to keep records up-to-date. In addition libraries consider electronic databases on computer-files such as CD-ROMs, a service similar to online searching or Selective Dissemination of Information (SDI), and not a library owned product. An example which supports this interpretation is the return policy which some electronic publishers

---

Anna M. Wang, Serials Cataloger, Ohio State University Libraries, 1858 Neil Avenue Mall, Columbus, OH 43210.

© 1988 by The Haworth Press, Inc. All rights reserved.

such as SilverPlatter require. When a current subscription is cancelled, the library must return all disks because access is permitted only under a subscription/lease arrangement.

The OCLC cataloging subsystem allows serial computer files to be cataloged using either the machine-readable data file workform or the serials workform as shown in Figures 1 and 2. Libraries must consider the intellectual nature of the materials, the print constants, indexing fields, and display on their online catalogs in order to make a decision as to which workform to use. If a library wishes to provide access to individual programs that are contained in a serial, separate analytic records can be created as shown in Figure 3. In Figure 3, line 13 exemplifies a linking entry to the serial (host item) that contains the component part.

In her article, "Microcomputer Software Cataloging: A Practical Approach," Susan Nesbitt predicts that user oriented cataloging may become the norm.[3] Indeed, catalogers must find creative ways to provide bibliographic and holdings information for local users. One possibility might be to provide minimum level cataloging for disks that the library leases, especially the disks that are funded by one-time money, and to provide full level cataloging for archival disks and disks that the library retains. (Some publishers such as Datext permit subscribers to retain disks.)

The Ohio State University Libraries do not catalog online databases or full-text journals which can be accessed online through DIALOG or BRS. This policy is followed despite the fact that the *Anglo-American Cataloging Rules, Second Edition, Chapter 9,* on *Computer Files (Draft Revision)* and the second edition of *Machine-Readable Data Files Format* do include cataloging rules for computer files available by remote access.

At the Ohio State University Libraries, the Collection Advisory Committee appointed a task force on CD-ROM which is working closely with the Task Force on Serials Management, the Work Group on Automated Reference Services, and the Cataloging Policy Advisory Council. Among its accomplishments thus far are a well-attended open meeting which was called in order to discuss cataloging policies and procedures, labeling, and the physical handling of CD-ROMs. As well as being very informative for our catalogers this meeting helped to determine cataloging policies and to

```
Screen 1 of 2
NO HOLDINGS IN OSU - FOR HOLDINGS ENTER dh DEPRESS DISPLAY RECD SEND
OCLC: 11215887        Rec stat: c Entrd: 841001       Used: 870410
Type: m Bib lvl: s Govt pub:    Lang: N/A Source: d Frequn: m
File: a Enc lvl: I Machine:  a Ctry: nyu Pub st: c Regulr: x
Desc: a Mod rec:    Dates: 1984-9999
  1 010
  2 040      OCL  c OCL
  3 019      12495334
  4 041  0   g eng
  5 090      b
  6 049      OSUU
  7 245 00   A+ disk magazine  h machine-readable data file
  8 260      New York, N.Y. :  b Ziff-Davis Publishing,  c 1984—
  9 265      A+ Disk Magazine, P.O. Box 2462, Boulder, CO, 80322
 10 300      program files on  computer disks ;  c 5 1/4 in. +  e  user's
manuals
 11 315      Nine issues yearly
 12 362 0    Vol. 1, no. 1—
 13 500      "A library of software programs for the Apple II, II+, IIe
computers."
 14 538      System requirements: Apple II, II+ or IIe; 48K; DOS 3.3.
 15 650  0   Computer programs  x Periodicals.
 16 740 01   A+disk magazine.

Screen 2 of 2
 17 740 01   A plus disk magazine.
 18 753      Apple II.
 19 753      Apple II+.
 20 753      Apple IIe.
```

FIGURE 1. These records are used with the Permission of the OCLC Online Computer Library Center, Inc.

```
Screen 1 of 2
NO HOLDINGS IN OSU - FOR HOLDINGS ENTER dh DEPRESS DISPLAY RECD SEND
OCLC: 11215949      Rec stat: c Entrd: 841001        Used: 861027
Type: a Bib lvl: s Govt pub:   Lang: eng Source: d S/L ent: 0
Repr:   Enc lvl: I Conf pub: 0 Ctry: nyu Ser tp: p Alphabt:
Indx: u Mod rec:   Phys med: z Cont:     Frequn: m Pub st: c
Desc: a Cum ind: u Titl pag: u ISDS:     Reguir: x Dates: 1984-9999
  1 010
  2 040    OCL  c OCL
  3 090    b
  4 049    OSUU
  5 212 0  A plus disk magazine
  6 245 00 A+ disk magazine h machine-readable data file
  7 246 30 A+disk magazine
  8 260 00 New York, N.Y. : b Ziff-Davis Publishing, c 1984-
  9 265    A+ Disk Magazine, P.O. Box 2462, Boulder, CO, 80322
 10 300    program files on computer disks ; c 5 1/4 in. + e user's
manuals.
 11 310    Nine issues yearly
 12 350    $179.00 for six issues
 13 362 0  Vol. 1, no. 1-

Screen 2 of 2
 14 500    "A library of software programs for the Apple II, II+, IIe
computers."
 15 500    System requirements: Apple II, II+, or IIe; 48K; DOS 3.3.
 16 650 0  Computer programs x Periodicals.
```

FIGURE 2

```
NO HOLDINGS
OCLC: 11222174        Rec stat: n  Entrd: 841003       Used: 841003
Type: m Bib lvl: a Govt pub:    Lang:  N/A Source: d Frequn: n
File: b Enc lvl: I Machine:   a Ctry:  xx Dat tp: s Regulr:
Desc: a Mod rec:    Dates: 1983,
 1 010
 2 040     OCL   c OCL
 3 090     b
 4 049     OSUU
 5 100 1   Winshell, Jason.
 6 245 10  Shape maker h machine-readable data file / c Jason Winshell.
 7 260 -   c
 8 300     1 program file on 1 computer disk ; c 5 1/4 in.
 9 500     Copyright 1983.
10 538     System requirements: Apple II, II+, or IIe; 48K; DOS 3.3.
11 520     Allows the user to create high-resolution graphics.
12 650 0   Computer graphics.
13 773 0   7 nnms t A+ disk magazine. g Vol. 1, no. 1. w (OCoLC)11215887
```

FIGURE 3

improve communication with other concerned parties so that the cataloging of CD-ROM materials is not being done in a vacuum.

It would be wonderful if each cataloger had a microcomputer workstation equipped with CD-ROM disk players and a printer. However, the reality is that the cataloging of computer files is almost always impeded by the lack of hardware in cataloging departments. Software has to be installed in a hard disk in order to obtain the bibliographic and holdings information necessary for cataloging. Who should install this? It is impossible for catalogers to have access to different kinds of hardware in order to load and read different computer files at one workstation. Without access to appropriate hardware cataloging may be based on the label of the physical carrier (cartridge, cassette, disk, etc.) and the accompanying documentation. However, computer files have variant titles and numeric designation changes just as printed and microformat serials do. As shown in Figures 4 and 5, the title on the title screen may vary from the disk label title, and the numeric or chronological designations may vary.

The ways in which disks are compiled also tend to complicate matters. Some issues may comprise one double-sided disk while other issues may be made up of one or more disks, as is shown in Figure 5. In order to expedite the cataloging process, the Ohio State University Libraries encourages departmental libraries to install their software and CD-ROMs and then to send printouts of the title screen, bibliographic, and holding information to the catalogers.

Since Apple Computer Incorporated unveiled its AppleCD SC CD-ROM drive on March 1, 1988, several vendors are in the process of developing new versions of CD-ROM products for use with this Macintosh microcomputer.[4] According to the *Bibliographic Input Standards*, 3rd edition, new cataloging records may be input in order to describe a different version of a software package. This means that if three departmental libraries subscribe to three different versions of the CD-ROM product, three separate bibliographic records may be called for. Alternatively, one could use one bibliographic record for both the IBM and Apple versions and then provide appropriate technical details and accompanying material notes for each version. Holdings of each version could be listed separately. For example:

Title: Challenge
Copy 1 Location: ENR 1985-1987 (IBM Personal System/2 version)
Copy 2 Location: REF 1985-1987 (Apple Macintosh version)
Copy 3 Location: BUS 1985-1987 (IBM PC XT version)

Listing the different versions in the holdings file may, in fact, be necessary since some database products such as CD/International and Compact Disclosure provide for the downloading of financial data to any of the wordprocessing and standard spreadsheet formats or to an ASCII file. Thus, a user needs to know what size diskette he should bring to the library in order to download information and what computers are compatible with the one that he uses.

CD-ROMs and other emerging optical disks are viable competitors for microforms because of their versatility, high data storage density and user-friendliness. I believe that CD-ROM complements but does not supplant paper and microforms. For instance, Datext's CD/International CD-ROM database provides quick and user-friendly access to financial and management information from the Worldscope database. However, to meet the needs of different users, Datext also provides full-text of report information in paper and microfiche formats. (See Figure 6, lines 30-32.) The CD-ROM product corresponds to: a five volume set of Worldscope Industrial Company Profiles; the International Annual Reports Collection on microfiche; and a printed Industry Index to the International Annual Reports Collection. It is important for libraries to provide analytical entries which link computer files to their online, paper, and microformat counterparts and vice versa. Thus, users will be able to use that medium which best serves their needs. (See Figure 7, lines 14, and 26-28 for an example.)

Tom Hendley predicts that it will be many years before CD-ROM will replace microformat for archival use or for the distribution of backruns of journals to libraries.[5] (We at Ohio State University have yet to handle the journals reproduced on CD-ROM.) In light of this one may well ask, "Is there a job left for serial catalogers?" My

FIGURE 4

```
Screen 1 of 3
OSU - FOR OTHER HOLDINGS, ENTER dh DEPRESS DISPLAY RECD SEND
OCLC: 14198161          Rec stat: c Entrd: 860909      Used: 880407
Type: m Bib lvl: s Govt pub:      Lang:   eng Source: d Frequn: q
File: d Enc lvl: I Machine:  a Ctry:  mau Pub st: c Regulr: r
Desc: a Mod rec:     Dates: 1986-9999
 1 010
 2 040        CPO  c CPO  d m/c  d CPO
 3 041 0      g eng
 4 090        L1028 b .E28
 5 049        OSUE  o nocir
 6 090        Z5811 b .U6883
 7 211 10     Educational Resources Information Center database
 8 245 00     ERIC database h computer file
 9 260        Boston : b SilverPlatter Information Services,
10 265        SilverPlatter Information, Inc., 37 Walnut St., Wellesley Hills,
MA 02181
11 300        computer laser optical disks ;  o 4 3/4 in.
12 315        Quarterly, with each disk being cumulative
13 362 1      Began in 1986.

Screen 2 of 3
14 500        "The ERIC (Educational Resources Information Center) database
consists of the Resources in Education (RIE) file of document citations and the
Current Index to Journals in Education (CIJE) file of journal article
citations."
15 538        System requirements: IBM PC, XT, AT, Personal System/2 Model 30 or
compatible; 512k; PC or MS DOS 2.1 or higher; 1 Philips, Hitachi, or Sony
compact disk drive; monitor; printer (optional)
```

```
16 500    Description based on: Jan., 1981-June, 1987; title from title
screen.
17 500    Disk label title: ERIC.
18 537    Resources in education (RIE) and Current index to journals in
education (CIJE).
19 538    Disk characteristics: CD-ROM.
20 500    Quarterly cumulations issued with set up and database disks (5 1/4
in. or 3 1/2 n.) and documentation.
21 500    Release 1.0 accompanied by 1 getting started booklet; 1 software
and printer installation guide; 1 quick reference card; 1 template; associated
documentation.

Screen 3 of 3
22 590    Library retains only the latest program disk and data disk.
23 650 0  Education x Research x Bibliography.
24 650 0  Education x Bibliography.
25 650 0  Education x Periodicals x Bibliography.
26 710 20 SilverPlatter Information Services.
27 710 20 Educational Resources Information Center (U.S.)   w on
28 740 01 ERIC.
29 730 02 Resources in education.
30 730 02 Current index to journals in education.
31 753    IBM PC    c DOS 2.1 or higher.
32 753    IBM PC XT c DOS 2.1 or higher.
33 753    IBM PC AT c DOS 2.1 or higher.
34 753    IBM Personal System/2 Model 30  c DOS 2.1 or higher.
35 910    b&yc880413
```

```
Screen 1 of 2
NO HOLDINGS IN OSU - FOR HOLDINGS ENTER dh DEPRESS DISPLAY RECD SEND
OCLC: 11135865       Rec stat: c  Entrd: 840910       Used: 860930
Type: m Bib lvl: s Govt pub:    Lang:  N/A Source: d Frequn: m
File: m Enc lvl: I Machine: a Ctry: lau Pub st: c Regulr: r
Desc: a Mod rec:    Dates: 1981-9999
  1 010
  2 040      OCL   c OCL   d TXI
  3 090      QA76.8.A6  b S3
  4 090      b
  5 049      OSUU
  6 245 00   Softdisk magazette  h machine-readable data file
  7 260      Shreveport, La. :  b Softdisk Magazette,  c 1981-
  8 265      Softdisk Magazette, 3811 St. Vincent, Shreveport, La. 71108
  9 300           data files,     program files on    computer disks :  b some sd.,
some col. ;  c 5 1/4 in.
 10 362 0   V. 1, #1 (Sept. 1981)--V. 3, [#6], Feb. 1984 ; No. 29--
 11 500     Cover display title: Softdisc.
 12 500     Editor: Jim Mangham.
 13 500     No issue for April 1982 or May 1983.

Screen 2 of 2
 14 500     Through Mar. 1983 each issue comprises one double-sided disk; from
Apr. 1983 on, each issue comprises two double-sided disks.
 15 538     Files include binary, Applesoft Basic, and text files.
 16 538     System requirements: Apple II (or higher); 48K; DOS 3.3; some
programs require additional peripherals.
 17 500     Description based on: V. 2, #5 and No. 29.
 18 650  0  Apple II (Computer)  x Periodicals.
 19 650  0  Microcomputers  x Periodicals.
 20 650  0  Computer programs  x Periodicals.
 21 700 10  Mangham, Jim.
 22 740 01  Softdisc.
 23 753     Apple II  c DOS 3.3.
```

FIGURE 5

answer is yes, but we will have to be more proficient in the handling of different media, especially since electronic publishing is here to stay. We will have to play an active role by voicing our opinions regarding the standards of bibliographic information for computer files as well as the integration of the MARC formats. We have to be sure that our voices are heard by the National Standards Organization (NISO) Compact Disc Format Committee and we must have representation in RTSD, LITA, RASD and MARBI (Machine-Readable Form of Bibliographic Information).

Cataloging computer files is challenging but not overwhelming. As Sheila S. Inter puts it, "The difficulty lies in learning to decipher the jargon, locate unfamiliar kinds of information."[6] Some sources which might be helpful include: the glossary included in the *Guidelines for Using AACR2 Chapter 9 for Cataloging Microcomputer Software* which was compiled prior to the emergence of optical technology; Bowers, Richard A., "Glossary for Optical Publishing," *The Optical/Electronic Publishing Directory* 1986: 10-24; "Glossary," *CD-ROM*, v. 2, ed. by Suzanne Ropiequet, John Einberger, and Bill Zoellick (Redmond, Washington: Microsoft Press 1987): 301-336; "Glossary of CD-ROM-Related Technical Terms and Acronyms," *Optical Information Systems* 6 (May-June 1986): 230-234.

It is important for serials librarians to equip themselves with the understanding of the impact of optical technology on library services and to get ahead of the laser edge. In April 1988, the Cataloging Department at the Ohio State University Libraries hosted the TECHNO-COM/CD-ROM Teleconference co-sponsored by ALA's Association of College and Research Libraries and CCAIT, the Community College Association for Instruction and Technology. It gave us an opportunity to learn what CD-ROM databases are available, how we can evaluate and integrate CD-ROMs into our library services in order to serve the needs of our patrons as best we can.

Computer files are on the rise. The scenario of electronic publishing for all secondary publications, for much of the primary literature, scientific and social sciences journals and for reference works by 1995 may come true, if it is technologically feasible[7] and if standards for electronic publishing are maintained. I look forward to

```
Screen 1 of 3
OCLC: NEW                 Rec stat: n Entrd: 880412        Used: 880412
Type: m Bib lvl: s Govt pub:     Lang:    N/A Source: d Frequn: m
File: m Enc lvl: I Machine:   a Ctry:  mau Pub st: o Regulr: r
Desc: a Mod rec:       Dates: 1987-9999
 1 010
 2 040     OSU  c OSU
 3 041 0   g eng
 4 049     OSU$
 5 090     HD2709 b .C3
 6 245 00  CD/International h computer file
 7 260     Woburn, MA : b Datext, Inc., c c1987-
 8 265     Lotus Development Corporation, 55 Cambridge Parkway, Cambridge,
Mass. 02142
 9 300          computer laser optical disks ; o 4 3/4 in.
10 315     Monthly, with disks being cumulative
11 362 0   Release 1 (Nov. 1987)-
12 500     "Contains the entire Worldscope database, which provides data on
approximately 5,000 companies listed on leading stock exchanges around the
world."

Screen 2 of 3
13 538     System requirements: IBM PC, PC XT, PC AT or compatible; IBM
monochrome or color display; 1 hard disk (1 megabyte hard diskspace); 1 floppy
disk; 640K; DOS 2.1 or higher; 1 Hitachi compact disk drive.
14 538     Optional hardware: 80-column or 132-column printer.
15 500     Title from disk label.
16 537     Worldscope.
```

FIGURE 6

17 500   All software is copyrighted by Lotus Developmet Corporation; the
Worldscope database is copyrighted by Wright Investors' Service (WIS); domestic
Worldscope data is compiled by WIS; and international Worldscope data is
compiled by the Center for International Financial Analysis and Research, Inc.
(CIFAR).
18 538   Disk characteristics: CD-ROM
19 500   Monthly cumulations accompanied by two installation floppy disks
(5 1/4 in.) and documentation.
20 500   Release 1 accompanied by 1 quick reference guide; 1 screening
reference guide; 1 Datext function key template; 1 CD/International user guide;
1 Datext reference guide.

Screen 3 of 3
21 650 0   Corporations, Foreign   x Finance   x Statistics.
22 650 0   Corporations, Foreign   x Management.
23 650 0   Corporations z United States   x Finance   x Statistics.
24 650 0   Corporations z United States   x Management.
25 740 01 CD international.
26 710 20 Datext, Inc.
27 710 20 Lotus Development Corporation.
28 710 20 Wright Investors' Service.
29 710 20 Center for International Financial Analysis and Research
(Princeton, N.J.)
30 730 02 Worldscope industrial company profiles.
31 730 42 The International annual reports collection.
32 730 02 Industry index to the International annual reports collection.
33 753   IBM PC   c DOS 2.1 or higher.
34 753   IBM PC XT   c DOS 2.1 or higher.
35 753   IBM PC AT   c DOS 2.1 or higher.
36 910   8yc880413
37 949 1   u PROGRAM DISKS VERSION 1   y 1987   u APR 1988 DATA DISK   y 1988

111

FIGURE 7

```
Screen 1 of 3
OSU
OCLC: 17784019      Rec stat: n Entrd: 880413      Used: 880413
Type: m Bib lvl: s Govt pub:      Lang: N/A Source: d Frequn: q
File: d Enc lvl: I Machine:  a Ctry: mdu Pub st: c Regulr: x
Desc: a Mod rec:   Dates: 198u-9999
 1 010
 2 040    OSU c OSU
 3 041 0    g eng
 4 090    Z6660 b .C58
 5 049    OSUv o nocir
 6 245 00 Compact Cambridge MEDLINE h computer file
 7 260    Bethesda, MD : b Distributed under license from NLM by Cambridge
Scientific Abstracts,
 8 265    Cambridge Scientific Abstracts, 5161 River Road, Bethesda, MD
20816
 9 300        computer laser optical disks ;  c 4 3/4 in.
10 315    Quarterly, with disks being cumulative and with annual cumulation

Screen 2 of 3
11 500    "MEDLINE provides access to worldwide biomedical literature,
including research, clinical practice, administration, policy issues, and
health care services. It corresponds to three printed indexes: Index Medicus;
Index to dental literature; [and] International nursing index."
12 538    System requirements: IBM PC, XT, AT, Personal system/2 Model 30,
or IBM compatible; 512K; 1 floppy and 1 hard disk drive or a 740k or larger
floppy disk system; Philips or Hitachi CD-ROM reader with interface card and
cable; Monochrome or color display monitor; printer; PC DOS or MS-DOS 3.1 or
higher.
```

```
13 500      Description based on: 1982; title from disk label.
14 537      MEDLINE
15 538      Disk characteristics: CD-ROM.
16 500      Quarterly cumulations issued with Compact Cambridge software disk
(5 1/4 in.) and documentation.
17 500      [Version] 2.1 accompanied by 1 Compact Cambridge user's manual.
18 650   0  Medicine x Periodicals x Indexes.

Screen 3 of 3
19 650   0  Nursing   x Periodicals x Indexes.
20 650   0  Veterinary medicine x Periodicals x Indexes.
21 650   0  Denistry  x Periodicals x Indexes.
22 650   0  Toxicology x Periodicals x Indexes.
23 650   0  Pharamacology x Periodicals x Indexes.
24 710  20  Cambridge Scientific Abstracts, inc.
25 710  20  National Library of Medicine (U.S.)
26 730  02  Index medicus.
27 730  02  Index to dental literature.
28 730  02  International nursing index.
29 753      IBM PC    c DOS 3.1 or higher
30 753      IBM PC XT c DOS 3.1 of higher
31 753      IBM PC AT c DOS 3.1 or higher
32 753      IBM Personal System/2 Model 30  c Dos 3.1 or higher
33 910      &yc880413
34 949   1  u PROGRAM DISK VERSION 2.1  y 1988  u 1982 Data Disk  y 1982  u
1983 Data Disk  y 1983  u 1984 Data Disk  y 1984  u 1986 Data Disk  y 1986  u
1987 Data Disk  y 1987
```

being able to carry an optical card memory version of the revised AACR2 and an optical disk that contains all the Cataloging Service Bulletins, Library of Congress Rule Interpretations, and an integrated MARC format to library conferences in the 1990s.

REFERENCES

1. L.R. Shannon, "New Look of Magazines," *The New York Times* Oct. 27, 1987: C11.
2. "CD-ROMs: the Laser's Edge in Data Storage," *Mechanical Engineering* 109 (Apr. 1987): 50-55.
3. Susan Nesbitt, "Microcomputer Software Cataloging: A Practical Approach," in *Cataloging Special Materials: Critiques and Innovations*, ed. Sanford Berman (Phoenix, AZ: Oryx Press, 1986), 25.
4. Roger Strukhoff, "Apple Joins the Corps," *CD-ROM Review* 3 (Mar/Apr. 1988): 14.
5. Tom Hendly, *CD-ROM and Optical Publishing Systems* (Westport, CT: Meckler Publishing Corporation in association with CIMTECH/BNBRF, 1987), 149.
6. Sheila S. Inter, "Problems and Solutions in the Descriptive Cataloging of Microcomputer Software," *Cataloging and Classification Quarterly* 5 (Spring 1985): 55.
7. F. Wilfrid Lancaster, Laura D. Drasgow, and Ellen B. Marks, "The Role of the Library in an Electronic Society," in *The Role of the Library in an Electronic Society*, ed. F. Wilfrid Lancaster (Urbana-Champaign, IL: University of Illinois Graduate School of Library Science, 1980), 174.

SELECTED BIBLIOGRAPHY

American Library Association. Committee on Cataloging: Description and Access. *Guidelines for Using AACR2 Chapter 9 for Cataloging Microcomputer Software*. Chicago: American Library Association, 1984.
American Library Association. RTSD/CCS Ad Hoc Subcommittee on Subject Access to Microcomputer Software. *Guidelines on Subject Access to Microcomputer Software*. Chicago: American Library Association, 1986.
Dodd, Sue A. *Cataloging Machine-Readable Data Files*. Chicago: American Library Association, 1982.
Dodd Sue A. and Ann Sandberg-Fox. *Cataloging Microcomputer Files: A Manual of Interpretation for AACR2*. Chicago: American Library Association,1985.
Holzberlein, Deanne. "Computer Software Cataloging: Techniques and Examples." *Cataloging and Classification Quarterly* 6 (Winter 1985/86): 1-83.

Inter Sheila S. "Problems and Solutions in the Descriptive Cataloging of Microcomputer Software." *Cataloging & Classification Quarterly* 5 (Spring 1986): 49-56.

Joint Steering Committee for Revision of AACR. *Anglo-American Cataloging Rules, Second Edition. Chapter 9, Computer Files (Draft Revision)*. Chicago: American Library Association, 1987.

Olson, Nancy B. *A Manual of AACR2 Examples for Microcomputer Software and Videogames*. Lake Crystal, Minn.: Soldier Creek Press, 1983.

Fatal Assumptions: Is There Light at the End of the Serials Tunnel?

INTRODUCTION

This morning, we want to focus on some different perspectives of the librarian/vendor/publisher interface. Our purpose is really to encourage discussion. This panel includes representatives from all three areas: libraries, vendors, and publishers, all together in one place at the same time, discussing largely the same issues. We've structured it so that each of us will speak, and then we'll open the floor up for questions.

Over the past years, there's been a general furor over journal pricing which has caused many of us to do some soul-searching both in terms of how libraries acquire materials and how publishers and vendors do business. Looking over reports produced by vendors and publishers to help my library do a better job with our materials budget, I've been struck by the fact that I repeatedly make assumptions about the structure of the information that we are being provided, and what can and cannot be done with it. I make assumptions as well about the method of packaging that information.

Just what do I mean? According to the *American Heritage Dictionary of the English Language*, an assumption is "a statement accepted or supposed true without proof or demonstration."[1] It may

---

Katina Strauch is Head, Collection Development, College of Charleston Library, Charleston, SC 29424.

Mary Fugle is Sales Manager for Libraries, Wholesalers and Journals, Springer-Verlag New York, 175 Fifth Avenue, New York, NY 10010.

Michael Markwith is Mid-Atlantic Regional Sales Representative, The Faxon Company, Westwood, MA 02090.

not surprise you to know that later definitions in the same dictionary talk about the Virgin Mary, heaven, and theology.

Seriously, what are some of the assumptions that we make about doing business in the current library acquisitions environment? Are they valid? Is it even appropriate in our environment for us to accept a "statement . . . without proof or demonstration"?

Over the next few minutes, I want to talk about two overall assumptions that we make in our acquisitions environment which we accept as "givens" (without proof or demonstration). If nothing else, I hope that this will get us to thinking and talking about assumptions that we make that maybe we shouldn't make. In order to do this, I'm going to introduce something that's only been mentioned cursorily at this NASIG conference: The Book!

First, there's the statement that *books and journals are different*. Let's examine that statement for a minute. Yes, books and journals are different in many ways: they are published differently; they are updated differently; bibliographically they are treated differently. And this isn't the end of the list. But I'm reminded of a book I read once called *The Rich Are Different*. People are different in many ways but they are also the same in many ways. Let's look at the ways that books and journals are the same, for just a minute.

From a mundane, stubbornly practical standpoint, books and journals are the same, i.e., they both contain information or knowledge. Both are produced by publishers from the work of authors. Both are sold for profit.

Why is it, then, that these two items, books and journals, need to be treated so differently by the publisher and the vendor?

As far as I can tell, it's because of packaging. We pay more for Crest toothpaste or a name brand author than we do for Eckerd's toothpaste or a unknown author because of the name and the packaging. Apparently, we pay more for journals than we do for books because the name of the journal is established and because it is packaged over continuous periods of time. Mary Fugle, the publisher representative on this panel, will say that we are paying for "the totality of a field of knowledge." The vendor says that we are paying for the service of additional operational support.[2] That may be. But in that case aren't we paying for more than just the bare information itself?

I'm sure that Mary and Mike will soon tear my comments apart, but just bear with me a little longer. The cost of producing a book and journal are the same, not so much in terms of volume as in terms of process. Both must be acquired from the author, both must be edited, typeset, and proofread, both must be marketed, distributed, and sold. In both cases, the publisher must bear many "upfront" costs in order to produce the information in its packaged form. I'm sure that you can all see where I'm leading. (Mary and Mike are rolling their eyes.)

Why, I ask (no longer the dewy-eyed child, but still curious), why do we have to pay the publisher and vendor "upfront" for journals if we're not doing the same for books? In fact, books are often longer and so there are more upfront costs. The costs are incurred at one time whereas the costs of producing a journal are spread out in the production of periodic issues. Also consider the fact that books can be returned to the publisher for credit up to six months after they are "bought." Have any of you ever tried to return *Chemical Abstracts* when it was six months old? How about the fact that you would be livid if you got an "added charge" bill for a book that you had received four months earlier? Yet we routinely swallow "added charge" price increases for journals because of the "exchange rate" or because "printing costs" have increased or because the "volume of scholarly output" is greater.

Now I know that Mary is going to madly and wildly defend this practice because she, after all, is a publisher, and I also know that Mike will basically side with her because he, after all, is a vendor. But that's not my perspective. I am a librarian and I have an obligation (to borrow from Marcia Tuttle writing in *LRTS*) to the library and library users.[3] When prices increase astronomically, I have to ask both the publisher and the vendor why. I also have to question their answers to my questions. I don't think the similarities between book and journal publishing that I am talking about can be totally dismissed. I think they at the very least need to be confronted and discussed.

The *second* assumption I want to talk about relates to *handling charges for journals*. Whereas I may be on shakier ground with this assumption (something which I really shouldn't admit), I still think that it's something to explore. The serials vendor seldom touches a journal unless it's for personal use, yet the book vendor handles books regularly. The book vendor has costs of shipping and handling of materials which the serials vendor does not have. The serials vendor gets discounts on particular types of journals which we never ask to be passed to us. Yet we expect the book vendor to pass on discounts to us. Still, the book vendor who charges for services rendered is frowned upon while we regularly negotiate with serials vendors for "the best" service charge. If there are any book vendors in the audience, you can take me to lunch later, but I can't help thinking that the more money we give the serials vendor upfront, the more we're prepared to give.

Once again, I put on my dewy-eyed sunglasses and ask, "Why?" Why are discounts and service charges so different for these two types of materials which both package information?

No doubt, there are many reasons for these practices. After all, it's always been done a particular way, so why change it, particularly if you're a vendor or a publisher? Perhaps there's the question of a monopoly and the fact that there are more book vendors out there than there are serials vendors and so there's more competition. Or maybe it's that the cost of automating data is more significant for the serials vendor than for the book vendor. Maybe, even, it's because I'm so ignorant of the workings of the book and serial vendors that I'm missing the whole point of their operations.

Still, I think that we should ask why. Why have these assumptions governing the purchase of books and journals been made? When did they start historically? Should we be making them? Maybe we can change something in our acquisitions environment. For a long time, we've been hearing from the vendors (especially) and the publishers (more recently) that we need to be more businesslike in our approach to acquisitions.

Now it's Mary's turn to talk and then Mike's, but I'm not going to let them have the last word.

Katina Strauch

REFERENCES

1. *American Heritage Dictionary of the English Language*. Boston: Houghton Mifflin, 1981, p. 80.
2. Rebecca T. Lenzini and Judith Horn, "1975-1985: Formulative Years for the Subscription Agency," *The Serials Librarian* 10:237 (Fall 1985/Winter 1985/86).
3. Marcia Tuttle, "The Serial Manager's Obligation," *Library Resources & Technical Services* 31(2):135-147 (April/June 1987).

RESPONSE

We have been presented with the assumption that books and journals are essentially the same thing, in that they both contain knowledge. From the publisher's perspective, that is where the similarity ends. Books and journals differ in terms of production, promotion, and editorial responsibilities. It is these differences I would like to discuss with you now.

The assumption that the publisher controls the flow of information is correct. The publisher disseminates information. When a book contract is signed, the publisher has an idea of the size and cost of the book but this can change by time of publication. For instance, 150 illustrations may become 300 illustrations and 50 colored plates, or 400 pages may develop into 700 pages. In addition, those of you who publish your own works or serve as editors know authors do not always adhere to deadlines. The two years we might expect for a scientific monograph from contract to publication may have to be extended. (A Springer record is 11 years!) Thus, the publisher often does not know what the product, i.e. monograph, will be like until going to press and cannot ask the customer to prepay for a product that does not exist. Historically, this has not always been true. Books at one time were only published by subscription, That is, a book was published only if a sufficient number of customers had paid for it in advance of publication. As publishing has developed into a business distinct from a "gentleman's profession," publishing houses are now able to assume the entire financial risk of publishing a monograph.

In *Managing the Serials Explosion*, David Taylor states "A Serial is a publication that first of all delivers on a promise. The second issue, which follows the first after a certain amount of time, creates the expectation for a third issue to come after a similar interval and to have a similar appearance and content. . . ."'Thus, a journal is a guaranteed product. Journal publishing mirrors scientific documentation. When a library subscribes to a journal, they are buying an entire field of knowledge which the publisher delivers in installments, i.e., issues.

A journal publisher makes a contract with an editor to find information worth disseminating. When the contract is signed, the editor and publisher agree on: the size of the journal, the number of pages, the number of issues, the content and arrangement, the price, and the publication of the first issue in approximately six months. The advance costs to produce this guaranteed product are enormous and include promotion, and editorial support for peer review, editing, secretarial support, etc. In general, the publisher invests in a journal for five years to recover these start-up costs, and would not consider publishing without subscribers. An information explosion in any STM field can and often does lead to expansion of writing and therefore papers to be published in journals. Hence, more cost and investment occur. The key difference in journal production is, once again reflecting the nature of scientific documentation, that journals are produced as fast as we can get an issue together.

As they provide documentation of an experiment or observation, papers must be published within six months or they are not of value.

A journal cannot fall behind schedule and all participants in the publishing process are very aware of schedules. Additionally, as journals are an ongoing entity, we are able to negotiate the best pricing from printers and typesetters.

As I have said, books can take a long time to publish, and usually receive only short term advance promotion. Not every book has the same importance. In fact, books are often promoted together by subject area. Books also have a distinct shelf life. Journals on the other hand are always an up-to-date source of information and are thus promoted very differently from books.

The promotion costs to launch a journal are many times greater than those to promote a book. From one discipline universe, we are looking for both authors and subscribers. To them we send a call for papers, subscriber mailings and space ads. Promotion must explain the aims and scope of the journal as well as highlight the reputation of the editors and the publisher. Both prospective authors and subscribers are purchasing an on-going concept. Inherent in the costs are sample issues sent for exhibition and in response to individual requests. This intense promotion continues for three years to keep the journal at the forefront of people's minds. Afterwards, we hope the journal can live on its own with minimal promotion.

Journals, be they scholarly or popular, are paid on a subscription basis. As with *Time, Newsweek, Vogue,* etc., our journals have a single issue price comparable to a newsstand price which is higher than the subscription price. Let's look at the administrative costs for invoicing for each issue of a journal. If we assume a publisher has 300 titles, each publishing 6 issues a year and having 900 customers per title, we are looking at 270,000 prepayment invoices. If we invoice for each issue we find ourselves cutting 1,620,000 invoices. These additional 1,350,000 invoices would arithmetically increase postage, staff and collection costs. Think of the additional costs to your own operation for cutting these checks. Think of the additional operations costs to your subscription agents. Clearly this is not a reasonable method of payment.

In this brief look at some of the differences between book and journal publishing I think you can see there are valid reasons for our methods of operation. If any of us seem to operate in the implied manner "because that's the way we've always done it . . . because that's the way it is . . ." it is that way after review and evaluation, the way we've always done it is still the best way to do it for now.

Mary Fugle

REFERENCE

1. Taylor, David Carson. *Managing the Serials Explosion*. Knowledge Industry Publications, Inc. 1982, p.7.

RESPONSE

The assumptions articulated by Katina clearly reflect the hot topics in the world of serials today. This is obvious from discussions at this and previous NASIG meetings, so I very much appreciate the opportunity to present the vendor's response to these assumptions about the commercial side of serials.

One of the ground rules forced upon us by Katina was "stay away from the same arguments that profits provide service, inflation increases costs, etc." Thus, I was forced to consider the questions of providing book and serial services to the academic library community and the resultant fees for providing these services in a broader context than I am used to espousing. Good, we are all tired of the same old platitudes, especially since some of us are paid to voice them everyday when we darken your doors! (I hope that some of my vendor colleagues, friends, and enemies alike, will feel free to comment during the discussion.)

Though based on my more than 20 years of experience in bookselling, library acquisitions and the world of serials, I hope that my presentation of the vendor's perspective will be a more global than personal one. I think we all realize that this is a tricky position at best and so Katina, Mary and I encourage your questions and comments. (For those of you who prefer a highly detailed and well-researched treatment of the business of journal publishing and the costs attendant to this business, I recommend the chapter by my colleague, Gary Brown, "The Business of Scholarly Journal Publishing" in the forthcoming monograph *The Business of Acquisitions* [Chicago: ALA, 1989?].)

My presentation will consist of two parts: the context in which we all work, live, and earn our daily bread; and my own assumptions about how the serials agent participates in the library/publisher/vendor relationship. I believe that although this is not a new topic, we must not forget that we have all chosen this profession over the selling, organizing, or producing of meaningless widgets. There may be more money in widgets, but there isn't more personal and professional value!

The structure and framework in which we all work, live, earn our daily bread, and have our being is the academic world. Publisher, serials agent and librarian serve together in the larger context of, and at the mercy of, academe. As the agent/vendor representative it is my assumption that the driving force in this world is the librarian. It is the librarian who drives our behavior, creates the need for products and services, and controls the behavior of our business relationship. Some may not want to acknowledge their accountability, and some may feel that this has all the earmarks of being condescending, but it is fact that the librarian is the consumer, the buyer, the client. The librarian dictates the nature of our relationship, but the system dictates the librarians' behavior. (Association quiz: what are the first things that come to mind when you hear the words: tenure; publish; perish; homeless?)

A few very simple questions that are at the heart of the structure and framework of academe include the following: Will researchers cease publishing the fruits of their labor? Can publishers refuse to publish this research? Will libraries cease buying the research? Isn't the academic world dependent on discovery, research, and sharing this information on a global basis with almost missionary zeal? I said that the questions were simple, but the answers are far too complex to resolve in this panel. Nevertheless, the context in which we operate is essential to why the assumptions, fatal though they be, continue to exist in the hearts and minds of librarians.

In the sixties, I was like many of you. I thought I would be a drum major for justice. Now I realize that I am a drummer for information. The vendor will continue to exist in the academic world as long as the system rewards research and there is sharing of this research with other scholars, students etc. Today it is journals, books, microfilm, microfiche, and some CD-ROM, electronic and desk top publishing, and some online databases. What was it 10 years ago or 50 years ago? What will it be in 10 years? I have no idea. I only know that as long as the research literature continues to expand, and is accessible through libraries, that there will be vendors to assist in the procurement and control of the information vital for research.

Many of you in this room have heard the anecdotal tragedy of why the village ice-man went out of business in the early 1900s. For those who do not know this story it is because the ice-man thought he was in the business of making ice, when he was really in the cooling business, refrigeration, not frozen water.

I suggest that if the librarian and the constituency he/she serves (scholar, student, etc.) were to say that they would accept all research on mimeographed paper, without fancy covers, advertising, and barcodes, that publishers would see the advantage to this remarkable new medium. Also, vendors would find ways to provide the services of consolidating information, billings, shipments, and other attendant clerical tasks to insure that the librarian received these materials needed by library users. But, would the information, research and the concomitant power of the research be available to the end user? That is the paradox we face in the world we have created for ourselves. The librarian drives the behavior of the publisher and the vendor, and the system drives the behavior of the librarian.

I know it is because I was a neophyte in this business in 1971 when Melcher published his work *On Acquisition* but I have always found the work to be informative and cogent. The chapter "How to Buy Serials at Best Advantage" is relevant despite being published 17 years ago. However, one word of caution and whimsy: do not take Melcher's cost figures literally. For example, he decries the inflated average price of a journal for academic libraries, "According to one experienced agent, the cost of an average journal is $16 and the cost of servicing library subscriptions runs about 10-12% of price . . . therefore, a title carrying no publisher discount might have a service charge of from $1.60 to $1.92."[1] As I said, the content is on target, but the figures are a bit whimsical if taken literally. However, the ratios and Melcher's portrayal of the entire acquisitions process, including the practical as well as theoretical, for books and serials, is valuable background reading for this discussion.

Another valuable resource for this discussion is Marcia Tuttle's article in the April/June 1987 issue of *LRTS*, an exceptional evaluation of our professional relationship as viewed by the "serials manager." What a great term! It makes sense. "Serials Manager," not Head of the Bibliographical and Serials Processing Component of the Electronic Information Center Division of the. . . ., "Serials Manager." In fact, her definition of why it is challenging and rewarding to be a library serials manager is something I use to explain my career move to serials.

> Successful serials management is a continuing challenge because of three trends: constant change in serial publications; runaway proliferation of journals and rising subscription prices; and the new technology applied to serials publishing, distributing, and processing. These developments have created an environment that requires knowledge and strong leadership by serials librarians.[2]

I would add vendors and publishers to those who must possess the required knowledge and must show strong leadership.

Vendors in the library or any service-oriented business do not create needs. They respond to them. This is in direct contrast to one point Marcia makes in her article (the only dispute I had with the entire work). She says, "Subscription agencies create 'needs' among their library customers, and they must market the new products and services successfully. They must respond to their customers' perceived needs in order to retain library business."[3] In my opinion, this is a fatal assumption as is Katina's "Well, it's just the cost of doing business." To both these assumptions I respond with an axiom that I have found true not only in our profession but in most of my personal business dealings as well. If you are satisfied with the service you receive you are paying enough. If you are dissatisfied with the service you receive, you are paying too much regardless of how much you are actually paying in real dollars.

I hope I have not been too simplistic, but in the ten minutes I have been allotted I am only trying to raise issues for discussion (and I was forbidden to use traditional arguments). However, I am very excited to note that in today's world of serials management there is a concept emerging which I hope becomes the basic assumption under which we all operate . . . the concept, or as Marcia states the "obligation" of partnership. "The serials manager's obligation to the library and library users is to become a full and equal partner in relationships with the subscription agent and the journal publisher. Partnership requires that the serials manager invest in a long term program of education, communication, and action."[4] This would not be a fatal assumption! Vendors welcome this partnership. We welcome the librarian into the business relationship. Marcia calls for equal status that is earned through continuing education, shared information from personnel in publishing and vendors, and knowledge of the basic distribution and marketing aspects of both publishers and vendors. Amen! Amen!

In response to both assumptions made by Katina, I offer the following comparisons between books and journals for academic libraries with their resultant service charge. The average discount for books, including trade, sci-tech, medical, paperback, university press, pamphlet, societal is approximately 25.8% for a representative order mix. The average discount for journals, including popular, societal, scholarly, university press, sci-tech is approximately 6.7% for the total subscriptions of an academic library. The significant difference in the pricing of a library's book orders vis-à-vis its serials orders, then, is that the bookseller recovers all operating costs from the publisher whereas the serials agent does not. It is incumbent upon the serials agent to act as an advocate for the libraries by working with publishers to reduce the publishers' costs to enter orders and to process claim reports. Furthermore, it is then incumbent upon the publisher to share these savings with the agent, and in turn the agent with the library.

I believe we have all been working on keeping costs under control, identifying high priced titles and inordinate percentage increases by title and publisher. How the vendor, librarian, and publisher responds to this data is central to what the partnership is all about. Understanding of the terms of doing business, hopefully establishes the trust and the freedom necessary so that we all can play our parts within the academic context.

Up to this point I have proudly avoided mentioning triangles, and all that is implied by triangular relationships. I do believe that it is true that in most instances, on most issues, two will team against one, or seem to team against one as perceived by that one. This is the nature of triangular relationships, personal or professional. However, while there will be points of disagreement the obligation that Tuttle calls for would assist dramatically in avoiding the majority of negative ramifications of the triangular relationship. My assumption is that the educated, communicative, and informed people, practicing active and real partnerships are willing to understand and share the emerging challenges of the information explosion age. It is also my assumption that publishers will work with vendors and librarians to produce what the library users need, and that the vendors will listen to librarians and publishers in order to expedite receipt and to assist in the control of the information regardless of format. In addition, librarians willing to be serials managers in the full meaning of the term will work with vendors and publishers to understand and participate in the determination of "costs of doing business" and will identify the resultant cost and labor savings in the management of their library. If this be truth, we will all have rewarding personal and professional lives.

I do think that most of the fatal assumptions of the commercial side of our serials management obligation can be overridden and replaced by the logical extension of the vendor's traditional role in the partnership. With the perspective of being in the middle, the vendor sees the strengths and weaknesses of both librarian and publisher (and vendor too) and wants to operate under the assumption of partnership, the partnership of the library serials manager, whether employed by the library, the vendor, or the publisher.

Finally, there are basic tried and true assumptions, "statements accepted or supposed true without proof or documentation," that govern the way every successful serials agent, vendor, or information broker in the western world operates. These assumptions are cliches and have been attributed in the oral tradition to the Harvard Business School:

— Never sacrifice the long-term (bottom line) for a short term gain;
— Always keep your ducks in a row;
— You can't shine meadow-muffins.

Michael Markwith

REFERENCES

1. Daniel Melcher and Margaret Saul, *Melcher on Acquisition* (Chicago: ALA, 1971), p. 151.
2. Marcia Tuttle, "The Serial Manager's Obligation," *Library Resources & Technical Services* 31:135(1987).
3. *Ibid.*, p. 140.
4. *Ibid.*, p. 142.

PANEL SUMMARY

I'm supposed to try to tie these three perspectives all together neatly so that they can be published for posterity in an ongoing scholarly journal. The fact that someone assumes that I can do that is in itself an assumption that should be questioned!

I'll take the easiest perspective first. The serials librarian is frazzled. Every day may hold a new, unexpected, demeaning invoice that will have to be dissected and explained to the powers that be. Whereas the vendor has all kinds of means of telling me what's happening and analyzing it once it's happened, the bottom line is that I have to translate all that either to my boss within the library or to the overall administration of my organization. And I don't look real good if I keep getting caught exceeding my budget.

Enter the subscription agent. The subscription agent needs my business. The subscription agent is trying hard to help me and still I'm asking for more. I want the subscription agent to have a crystal ball and tell me exactly what my costs are going to be. I don't want any surprises. If I have too many, I may quit subscribing to journals which will cut down on the vendor's income. This threatens the vendor's market share and may help the competition. The vendor wants to please me, but the cost of a journal is beyond the vendor's control.

Enter the publisher. The publisher can help both the librarian and the subscription agent. The publisher controls the cost of the journal. But the publisher has the same profit motive as the vendor. The library can run in the red and someone may get fired. Nonetheless if the journal loses too many subscribers, it may have to cease publication. Similarly, if the subscription agent loses too many customers, the subscription agent may be faced with ceasing publication as well.

This is why the triangular relationship between library/publisher/subscription agent has a chance of succeeding. The library needs access to information. The subscription agent wants the library to have access to that information because it increases the agent's profit. The publisher, as well, wants the library to have the information contained in its journal so that it can continue publishing the journal.

Everything is copacetic. We need to keep talking. I have a greater respect for both the vendor's and the publisher's role than I did before this panel started. I hope Mary and Mike can say the same thing about their perspectives, and I think this comes from asking each other why.

Katina Strauch

An Overview of Current Developments in the Bibliographic Control of Serials

Ed Jones

SUMMARY. A personal view of current developments in the bibliographic control of serials, including AACR 2, harmonization of bibliographic practice across national frontiers, CONSER, US-MARC bibliographic format integration, the Linked Systems Project, the multiple versions question, and the International Serials Data System.

What I'm going to do here is touch on the high points, which means that I will inevitably oversimplify. So bear in mind that everything I'm telling you is much more complicated than I make it out to be.

I'll start with the mundane: the cataloging code. Now, it's a commonplace in some circles that AACR 2 is *IT*, that there will be no new codes from here on out—just fine-tuning of a near-perfect instrument. Well, maybe. Certainly by requiring AACR 2 to conform, more or less, to the stipulations of a growing number of international conventions—primarily the 1961 Paris Principles and the family of ISBDs—our field of action has become much more circumscribed. I think we are much more likely to see a constant, if gradual, evolution of AACR 2 rather than its replacement by AACR 3. The period of revolution is behind us, and the counter-revolution is now pretty much limited to a guerilla action at Northwestern.

In an Anglo-American context, we moved some seven years ago from the two editions of AACR 1—one North American and one British—to the one edition of AACR 2 (along with three or four

---

Ed Jones, Senior Cataloger for CONSER and Preservation, Harvard University Library, Cambridge, MA 02138.

national sets of rule interpretations and optional provisions to make things interesting). Is this progress? I think so. I hope that in a few years, driven by increased demand for a *useful* international exchange of MARC records, the differences among national interpretation will be sufficiently reduced so that we can begin to build a common Anglo-American authority file.

Progress is being made in this area, but any agreements across national frontiers involve the relinquishing of a degree of national sovereignty. And national sovereignty is something one is loath to part with, especially when favorite rule interpretations hang in the balance. But we are doing it, slowly.

At some point in the future we will enjoy a common data base of American, Canadian, British, Australian, and New Zealand bibliographic and authority records. This will be only the first and easiest leg of a hard journey. Farther on will lie the formidable challenge of the non-English-speaking world. I know we don't like talking about this much, but if we are to share bibliographic and authority records with that world, we will have to come to some sort of accommodation with it. I don't think we will be able to convince them to catalog in English. What is more likely is that we will all agree to apply one simple overriding rule when dealing with items in different languages: that the language of the text governs the language of the catalog record. This will allow a relatively painless sharing of descriptive cataloging. However, it will mean giving up unified files for corporate names and replacing them with multiple interconnected files—not really as awful as it sounds. It will also mean multiple bibliographic records for bilingual and multilingual works. (Libraries would presumably choose the record or records most appropriate to their own linguistic community.)[1] Pretty scary. But this will orient the catalog record towards the likely end-user: the speaker or reader of that language.

If past experience is anything to go on, such developments lie comparatively far in the future. Unfortunately, we are already confronting large files of foreign records—UKMARC, CANMARC—in our bibliographic utilities long before we have made the agreements (and concessions) necessary to facilitate their use. To bring things even more down to earth, in CONSER, we're still trying, after seven years of AACR 2, to harmonize U.S. and Canadian practice.

CONSER has been going through changes.[2] After reports, retreats, and convocations of elders, we have a new definition of what the acronym stands for, and we have a new governance structure that has made some substantive changes possible as well. CONSER is enjoying a period of growth in membership and is beginning to look beyond its traditional (since 1981) preoccupation with current serials cataloging towards larger questions, such as retrospective conversion, format integration, the Linked Systems Project, and the murky Multiple Versions Question.

USMARC format integration is an idea that has been discussed in a desultory way for some time. Now it's being discussed earnestly, by ALA's MARBI Committee.[3] The format integration proposal[4] is actually three proposals: first, that variable-length datafield content designators be validated for all forms of material (meaning, "If the shoe fits, wear it" — if a serial has characteristics of a sound recording, it's OK to use the relevant sound recording tags); second, that a repeatable fixed-length datafield (the 006 field) be defined for "additional material characteristics" (that is, other than those encoded in field 008, and meaning, from the serialist's point of view, that a serial can also be something else, and something else can also be a serial [but more of that later]); third, that certain data elements currently defined in the format be deleted or labelled obsolete. (This is something not really required for format integration but the feeling was, while we're at it, why not?) These proposals taken together will effectively "integrate" the seven existing USMARC formats into a single all-purpose format.

Of course, if MARBI could just throw out all the existing formats and start again from scratch, the resulting integrated format would no doubt look quite different. But the need to accommodate the accumulated store of millions of existing USMARC bibliographic records limits the available options.

How will all this affect serialists? Well, one of the effects of format integration will be to permit the handling of the serial aspects of any type of material, without the loss of detail relating to other aspects. For instance, you will be able to encode a serial audiocassette as an audiocassette in field 008, while encoding serial fixed field data elements in field 006 (or vice versa), and you will be able to use the variable fields appropriate to each aspect in a single record. (I won't get into the question of what such a record represents *really*? — that is, is it a serial audiocassette or an audiocassette serial? This is a question of some interest in CONSER, but it need not bother us here.)

I also won't talk about how these records will be shared. Such talk inevitably leads to talk of the much-talked-about Linked Systems Project (LSP), which I will now talk about. Most catalogers are aware of LSP as the means by which the OCLC and RLIN copies of the LC/NACO authority file are now kept up-to-date. Likewise, catalogers at NACO libraries are beginning, via LSP, to contribute name authority records to LC through their OCLC and RLIN terminals. A serials application of LSP would provide an ideal method for non-OCLC CONSER libraries — as well as non-North American *would-be* CONSER libraries waiting in the wings — to indirectly access and contribute to the CONSER database on OCLC. But while desirable, such an application will probably come later rather than earlier in LSP's development, despite our fond wishes. It looks like monographs will have priority. So for the time being we are seeing more prosaic methods for expanding CONSER participation, primarily through what I call "CONSER participation by proxy" (where a non-OCLC CONSER institution provides the cataloging, and the NST section at LC provides the inputting). LSP, nevertheless, remains the long-term dream.

The Multiple Versions Question is more of a near-term dream. It has received a lot of press over the last few years,[5] and CONSER now has a task force focusing on it.

What are multiple versions? Well, that's part of the task force's charge. But for our purposes, I'll hazard my own definition: a work exists in multiple versions when the content of the work remains the same but the carrier varies. By this definition, reproductions in macroform and microform probably represent multiple versions, as would VHS and Beta versions of videocassettes, IBM PC and Apple Macintosh versions of microcomputer software, sound recordings on vinyl disc, audiocassette, and CD. However, dubbed, subtitled, and colorized versions of motion pictures probably would not. It depends on how much is content and how much is carrier.

An answer to the multiple versions question would be a Good Thing. Among the perceived benefits of an answer would be the ability to eliminate or suppress redundant data in online public catalog displays. For example, if your library holds both VHS and Beta versions of a videocassette, it would be nice to be able to tell the user this with one record rather than two. The question then becomes how best to achieve this: (1) through a single bibliographic record with embedded data about all available versions? (2) through a single "generic" bibliographic record, with version-specific data relegated to holdings records? (3) through a multi-tiered approach, with version-specific data contained in a new type of record intermediate between the bibliographic record and the holdings record? or (4) through multiple version-specific bibliographic records, with one record designated as a "focal" record and the other records pointing towards it via a special control-number field?

Each of these multiple answers has implications for communication, for the USMARC format, for international tape exchange, and for the cataloging code. And I expect it is these implications that will drive the discussions and ultimately determine the choice among the answers.

In CONSER, the U.S. Newspaper Project (USNP) chose long ago among these answers.[6] They chose answer number 2. There, a single bibliographic record—the "master record"— describes the paper copy (even when the paper copy no longer exists) and version data is relegated to holdings records. If a different answer is implemented by CONSER, then the USNP choice may need to be reexamined. Given the large number of records involved, it may be decided to "grandfather" this class of records.

In terms of its own house, CONSER has been sweeping up lately. There are now experimental guidelines for record creation and maintenance. This is not to say that there were no guidelines before, but it was more of an oral tradition. We have also given a tentative nod to retrospective conversion, including, under certain circumstances (gulp!), latest-entry catalog records. No one has yet ventured to undertake a serial retrocon project within this framework—perhaps the curse that "all serial retrocon projects become serial recataloging projects" holds them back—but the guidelines are there for them that dare.

Finally, ISDS. Much of what I have been talking about relates to CONSER. And this may lead you, as it sometimes does me, to say, "Is there anything beyond CONSER?" Well, there is. There's the International Serials Data System, the Interpol of the serials world. ISDS represents, for better or worse, the international solution to serials bibliographic control.[7] The ISSN has become the ubiquitous symbol of ISDS, appearing on serials the world over, regardless of language or script. Aside from automation, it may be the best thing that's happened to serials check-in in years.[8]

But here I want to look at it from a cataloging point of view. In the ISDS register, and those national files that have adopted the same methods, the ISSN is the control number, linked to a key-title (a sort of internationally agreed-upon uniform title) that serves as the main entry. For U.S. and Canadian serials entered under title, AACR 2 usually agrees with ISDS. For other serials, however, there is much greater variation between the two, brought on by the use of different romanization schemes, different rules for formulating qualifiers, and so on.

At present, CONSER and ISDS are in a state of peaceful coexistence, each with a growing arsenal of records. But sooner or later we will have to reach an accommodation with them in our serials cataloging practice: it is ISSNs, after all, that are appearing on all our serials, not LCCNs. The challenge will be to reconcile AACR 2 rules for serial entry and uniform title construction with ISDS stipulations for key-title construction, while retaining some sense of philosophical coherence (we have already gone a long way towards reconciling rules for serial title change). The problem is, we don't want to get too far away from the AACR 2 principle of treating all categories of materials equally in terms of choice and form of entry. What I can see us ultimately doing is deciding to fudge it, through some new rule that chooses entry under "internationally prescribed citation forms" — a code-phrase for key-titles — in preference to entry according to the other provisions of the code.

I've ranged over a wide ground here. If I have an overriding theme in reviewing these developments (and I may not), it is the growing interrelationship between everything and everything else, especially between national and international developments. In a way, we long ago hitched our wagon to the international star, but we are only slowly coming to grips with all that implies.

NOTES

1. This is very close to the Canadian solution for works in English and/or French. See Wayne Jones and John Clark, "Bilingual Serial Cataloguing at the National Library of Canada," *Serials Librarian* 12 (1987): 53-62.

2. Jeffrey Heynen and Julia C. Blixrud, *The CONSER Project: Recommendations for the Future*, Washington: Library of Congress, 1986.

3. See summary in *LITA Newsletter* 9 (spring 1988): 19.

4. "Proposal 88-1: Format Integration," available from the Cataloging Distribution Service, Library of Congress, in its USMARC Format: Proposed Changes subscription service.

5. See especially Dan Lacy, "Libraries in an Age of New Technology," *LCPA Newsletter* 19 (July/Aug. 1987): 4-5; Crystal Graham, "Rethinking National Policy for Cataloging Microform Reproductions," *Cataloging and Classification Quarterly* 6 (summer 1986): 69-83; *Cataloging Titles in Microform Sets*. Report of a Study Conducted in 1980 for the Association of Research Libraries by Information Systems Consultants, Inc. Richard W. Boss, Principal Investigator. Washington, D.C.: Association of Research Libraries, 1983, pp. 29-32, 56-61.

6. Robert B. Harriman, "Coordination of Cataloging Practices in the United States Newspaper Program," *Cataloging and Classification Quarterly* 6 (summer 1986): 23-24.

7. For examples of the spread of ISDS records as the basis of national catalog records, and of key-title as the choice of entry, see Sten Hedberg, "Serials Cataloguing in Sweden," *Serials Librarian* 12 (1987): 11-17; Christian Lupovici, "Le catalogue collectif national des publications en série, "Bulletin des bibliothèques de France 29 (1984): 420-431; and the series of numbered card summaries, *Applications*, issued by ISDS and available in the U.S. through the National Serials Data Program, Library of Congress.

8. The primacy of the ISSN is likely to be reinforced if there is widespread acceptance by serial publishers of the biblid (ISO 9115: 1987), an ISSN-based bibliographic strip used to identify both individual issues of serials and individual contributions in serials and books. Biblids may be present on publications in both eye-readable and machine-readable forms, to facilitate automatic check-in (e.g., by light pen). The code developed in the U.S. by SISAC and NISO (draft ANSI Z39.56-198X) represents a compatible augmented version of the biblid.

WORKSHOP SESSION REPORTS

Serials Pricing: The Impact of Exchange Rates and Currency Trends

Cindy Hepfer

Con Jager, North American Area Manager for Martinus Nijhoff International, opened the Serials Pricing workshop by depicting the serials vendor as middle man, caught between equally frustrated foreign publishers and North American librarians. What librarians want, he indicated, is to obtain foreign journals at the best possible price and without risk. It is the vendor's task to strike the best deal for clients.

Three exchange rate policies for Eurotitles were outlined. The "rate of date" system fixes the exchange rate on the date an invoice is paid. This is the riskiest system, since if the dollar declines, the library pays more. Second is the "preset publisher rate" whereby the publisher presets a rate for a few months but may impose added charges later on if the dollar drops. Finally there is the "vendor rate." This is the safest method for the librarian, as the vendor purchases futures contracts from a bank and, in effect, gambles

---

Cindy Hepfer, Head, Serials and Bindery, Health Sciences Library, Abbott Hall, SUNY at Buffalo, Buffalo, NY 14214.

© 1988 by The Haworth Press, Inc. All rights reserved.

many months in advance on a fluctuating exchange rate. The librarian can thus proceed with budget planning, but should be aware that the process is a costly one for the vendor.

Jager admitted that there is no "best" answer to the exchange rate problem. He urged librarians both to take advantage of prepayment plans to cost cuts and to check with their vendors about exchange rate practices. Finally, a prayer for a strong and stable dollar was suggested.

Next John Tagler, Director of Marketing Services for Elsevier Science Publishers, cogently and calmly attempted to explain why foreign publishers have become scapegoats for librarians' budget woes. He showed a chart depicting the relationship of the U.S. dollar and the Dutch guilder from 1944 through 1987. Until 1970, the dollar remained relatively stable, and so exchange rates were not a consideration for budget planning. During the 1970s, however, the dollar weakened, stabilized and rebuilt, peaking in 1985 at a post-war high and then dipping by 1987 to a post-war low. Thus the exchange rate has become a major factor to consider in library budget planning.

Tagler went on to outline two other factors affecting journal pricing. These were the exponential growth of scientific information and the resulting expansion in the number of volumes published per year. The King study showing that the amount of scientific information doubles every 15 to 17 years was cited, as were statements that in the fields of neurology and immunology alone, scientists have learned more in the past five to ten years than in all the rest of history. Two case studies were offered to illustrate the exchange rate/publication growth problems, *Journal of Crystal Growth* and *Journal of Chromatography*.

According to Tagler, library budget increases have generally been reasonable in terms of covering general inflation, but have not been sufficient to cope with radical swings in currency exchange or the fantastic growth in scientific research. Differential pricing was also addressed. Tagler pointed out that the four Elsevier branches each price in domestic currencies. The Dutch and Swiss branches have one worldwide price. The British and American branches do likewise but add a surcharge for shipping. Libraries pay for Elsevier titles by using the value of domestic currencies at the time of payment. These rates are set by banks which give no break for "the free flow of information."

Discussion was both cordial and informative. When asked what librarians should retain from this workshop, Jager replied that they should separate the exchange rate issue from price increases in order to understand what publishers are really doing. Tagler's response was that there is simply more information available than libraries can afford to buy. Information on how cancellations affect the price of a title for those libraries still subscribing was requested. Tagler said that it would be hard to formulate a single answer as the journals with large circulation are not so much affected as ones with a small circulation. He pointed out that Elsevier has not yet raised the price of any of the large circulation journals to compensate for cancellations. He also discussed Elsevier's response to the growth of *Journal of Chromatography* which was split into two separately purchasable sections in order to stem the tide of cancellations.

Another hot topic which surfaced was the maximum discount of 10% to vendors which Elsevier and Karger have recently set. Tagler said the Elsevier cap is on 7 journals and 3 Excerpta Medica titles, and that approximately $300 should be sufficient to cover all vendor processing fees. Jager added that while all of the vendors still want to handle the "very good" Elsevier package, the slimmer margin is causing relationships among the vendors to become less friendly.

The final comment of the workshop came from the Cambridge University Press representative who talked about differential pricing as a means of avoiding exchange rate swings and as providing prices more reflective of a local market. Tagler rejoined that the U.K. has a significant home market, while the Dutch Elsevier exports almost exclusively and thus does not realize the same advantages.

Getting Started with the USMARC Format for Holdings and Locations

Daphne Hsueh

Greg Anderson, Systems Librarian, University of Georgia, was the leader of this workshop. His presentation was divided into four broad sections: history of the format; its special features; its structure; and his experience with its implementation.

The development of the format was first undertaken by a consortium of southeastern universities. Their initial goal was to devise a computer notation for serial holdings which would facilitate control. Later, with the involvement of the Library of Congress, the project became an effort to develop a standard to communicate holdings and locations information.

Being a communications format, the USMARC Format for Holdings and Locations belongs to the growing family of MARC formats. However, it possesses certain characteristics that set it apart from the other members of the family. Unlike other MARC formats which carry universal data elements, such as the one for books or serials, the format for holdings and locations communicates information unique to a particular library's holdings.

When linked to a particular bibliographic record this format enables individual libraries to express their holdings in a linear form while actually being controlled in a hierarchical form. Anderson emphasized that this format does not address the question of display. A library could extract the information and then manipulate the data to build a desired display, as long as it used the holdings and locations format to code the necessary data. The use of this format also facilitates any union listing project.

Daphne Hsueh, Head, Serials Cataloging, Ohio State University, Main Library, Columbus, OH 43210.

© 1988 by The Haworth Press, Inc. All rights reserved.

Although this format is often used to communicate holdings and locations information for serial publications, it is a standard for communications meant to be used with other forms of publication as well, monographic series or multi-part publications etc.

With the aid of handouts and transparencies, Anderson explained in some detail the basic structure of the format including fields and code values. While component parts, such as leader information and directory, are common among all MARC formats, the fields that carry holdings data form the core of this format.

Anderson pointed out that fields in the core section work in pairs. One field (e.g., 853) serves as a controlling factor, while its corresponding partner (e.g., 863) expresses its content. Such an arrangement was derived from the concept that information in the controlling field is nationally valid (e.g., the publication pattern of a serial) whereas that in the contents field (e.g., the holdings) is derived locally. It is in this core section that the desirable feature of the format, compressibility/expandability, comes into play. Compression, Anderson explained, is the act of taking data, looking for gaps, and squeezing the data into a more manageable arrangement. Expansion, as the word indicates, is the very opposite of compression. Expansion, though not essential for display design, was essential for system design because of its implication for predictability, a factor crucial in any check-in design.

The format also provides a field (866) to list an irregular pattern, a kind of free-text field. Compared to the dynamic nature of field 863, the 866 field could be considered static. Data in this field is not subject to manipulation. However, through the use of sequence control numbers a combination of pattern holdings and irregular holdings can coexist side by side so that the complete run of a serial that a library holds might be listed.

The USMARC Format for Holdings and Locations offers a range of options. Due to this demand for making choices it initially may appear very formidable, particularly in a workshop setting. However, Anderson assured everyone that after some hands-on experience, it would be far less formidable.

The experience of using this format in the University of Georgia Libraries was briefly described. After careful training library assistants were used to create pattern information. Holdings data gathered from various sources, in order to keep checking in the stacks to a minimum, was then input.

Anderson concluded his presentation by pointing out that such a standard promotes the exchange of holdings information, and that it makes a library less wedded to a specific system. He also reminded everyone that further development of the standard would be in order once more libraries have had some experience using it. Suggestions for refinement could be made at that time.

Serials Snags, or, What to Do with Unsolicited Receipts and Partners in Serials Access: Cooperation Between Technical and Public Services

Marjorie E. Bloss

Two papers comprised this workshop, each dealing with a very different aspect of serials. Both papers, however, focused on the day-to-day procedures and practices experienced in their authors' libraries.

Patricia Ohl Rice (Pennsylvania State University) described the problems caused by what she called "snags." The term refers to any item (serial or not) for which no order can be identified. Included in her definition are invoices for which no purchase order could be identified. Penn State's rule of thumb was "if they could figure out why they got it, it wasn't a snag."

Although Penn State uses FAXON's SC-10 for serials check-in, Rice decided to use Penn State's locally based OPAC, LIAS (Library Information Access System) for her snag project instead. Her decision was based on cost considerations. Although LIAS does not directly interact with the FAXON system, both databases can be accessed on an IBM XT through a hard drive database manager.

Rice initiated the Snags Project from a card file of more than 2,000 titles. This card file had all the negative features of a manual

---

Marjorie E. Bloss, Manager, Resource Sharing Department, OCLC, Inc., 1428 Park Ridge Drive, Worthington, OH 43235.

© 1988 by The Haworth Press, Inc. All rights reserved.

file. The record structure that was designed for this project in the MICROLIAS system contains abbreviated cataloging information. Because the database can be searched by keyword, form of entry was not crucial. Since those doing the searching were not necessarily librarians, this feature was essential.

In addition to being able to identify titles for which no purchase order had been generated, the snag record also included fields for routing/decision-making purposes. At the end of the month, a "tickler" file could be printed in order to remind staff to make their retention decisions and return the items in question.

Rice concluded her presentation by identifying some of the problems Penn State experienced with the snag process. The first are administrative; namely, that no one librarian is fully in charge of the Snags file and snag procedures are not yet integrated into unit routines. The second problem is more conceptual in that the Snags database is not totally integrated into the two major databases used by the library—LIAS and FAXON. Even so, the creation of the Snags file has eliminated the vast majority of the paper snags file from more than 2,000 titles to a little more than 200.

Elaine Rast's portion of the workshop entitled "Partners in Serials Access: Cooperation between Technical and Public Services" traced the reorganization of both Technical and Public Services Departments at Northern Illinois University (DeKalb) over a sixteen-year period. In large part, these reorganizations occurred because of budget cuts. Structurally, however, it was the staff, guided by Rast's enthusiasm, who decided to have the professionals in technical services provide assistance in public service areas.

A number of Rast's statistics point toward a strong basis for this decision. She cited that approximately 60-80% of libraries' budgets are spent on serials. Serials form the bulk of reference questions (75%), with approximately 55% of these questions answered. Some 15% of the questions are not answered due to patron error. A staggering 35% of the serial items held by and requested in a library were not found because of library-related problems (shelving problems, too many locations, etc.).

In order for restructuring to transpire, considerable responsibility was placed on the paraprofessional, Library Technical Assistant (LTA) staff for the cataloging and classifying of materials. This required a highly trained and educated staff. As Rast pointed out in the discussion period, the vast majority if not all of Northern's LTAs are college graduates.

The use of technical service staff provided considerable cross-fertilization of information between technical and public services staffs. Technical services staff found themselves informing their public services colleagues of cataloging rules, rule interpretations and internal decisions. Public services staff found themselves becoming more and more knowledgeable when it came to interpreting bibliographic records and locating materials within the library.

An automated circulation system, LCS, linking 30 academic libraries in Illinois, is used by Northern not only for circulation but for On Order and Binding information as well. These, then, were additional areas where the technical services staff could interpret data for public services. With the creation of a statewide online catalog, ILLINET ONLINE, technical services staff will be able to provide even more assistance in their public services capacities.

With regard to the future, Rast feels that there are more similarities than differences between technical and public services duties. She envisions a new age of professionalism in which technical and public service responsibilities will continue to blur, for the underlying theme in all library tasks is serving the public.

Research Methods for Analyzing Serials Budgets

George Lupone

Deana Astle, Clemson University, and Charles Hamaker, Louisiana State University, led this workshop. The purposes of the workshop were to present reasons for monitoring serials budgets, to outline the causes of sharp price increases, and to provide new methods of analyzing budgets. These were achieved through the presentation of two case studies which were done by Astle and Hamaker at Clemson and Louisiana State Universities, respectively.

In addressing the reasons for monitoring budgets, Astle pointed out that the consequences of rising serials costs for many libraries were cancellation of serial titles and reduction in the dollar amount spent on non-serial materials. Through monitoring, better predictions of expenditures were possible. Identification of "predator" titles, those which increased rapidly in price and were very expensive, became possible. Monitoring also provided data which was used to educate faculty, library and university administrations about serials issues. The data allowed the university communities to make informed decisions about the management of serials collections.

Several factors have contributed to the high annual increases in serial prices over the last few years. The rapid two-year decline in the value of the dollar against foreign currencies was an important factor. At Clemson University, thirty-five percent of the serial titles were from overseas. Discriminatory pricing, primarily by British publishers, was also a factor. Although this practice was thought to be in abatement, British publishers have recently been charging a higher price to the U.S. market. In addition, Hamaker talked about

---

George Lupone, Assistant Director for Access Services, Cleveland State University Libraries, Cleveland, OH 44115.

"cash cows" in the serials publishing trade, i.e., titles which provide steady income to publishers over a period of time. Analysis of titles by three vendors showed that these titles were initially expensive and that they increased greatly in price each year. Twenty-three percent of the price increase for the publishers under analysis came from only six percent of their titles. The monopolistic nature of the industry also contributed to high prices for serials. Each serial contains unique information which cannot be obtained elsewhere. The pressure on university faculty to publish, and the captive library market which must buy the scholarly research, only serve to fuel the inflationary cycle.

An underlying concern at both Louisiana State University and Clemson University was that traditional subject approaches for understanding and analyzing serials collections were not providing all the necessary data. Astle and Hamaker found that looking at serials budgets sorted by publisher and country-of-origin added a dimension which began to illustrate the spiraling serials pricing problem. With data in hand, faculty and administrators were better able to exercise control over the serials collection.

Louisiana State and Clemson both performed computer analyses on serials pricing data. LSU used SAS on a mainframe while Clemson used a spreadsheet program on a microcomputer. Both presenters stressed that gathering and inputing data was not time-consuming and that time spent was well-justified by the results. It would take student help and/or staff two to three weeks, working eight hours per day, to collect data for 2,000 titles. Initially, both institutions collected data for titles costing more than $200. Later, Clemson collected data for titles costing $100 or more and LSU for titles $80 or more.

Faxon's country-of-origin management report served as the initial source of information. It provided title, country-of-origin, and cost data. Because the intent of the Faxon report and the universities' budget analyses were different, some information provided by the vendor had to be checked. For example, the country-of-origin listed on Faxon's report was often the country of their source or of a distributor, not the country of publication. In addition, the prices on the report were sometimes two-year prices instead of the annual prices. Publisher data and the local call number were not included on Faxon's report. Consequently, in order to fill in missing information, data had to be found in Faxon's database, the online catalog, *Ulrich's*, local records, and the publication itself. Finding the most recent publisher was the most difficult task.

With the information gathered and entered into a computer, it was then possible to manipulate it. Sorts by publisher were used to determine the impact of a particular publisher on the collection. Sorts by country-of-origin were useful in finding out how much would be spent in various currencies, a very helpful report for predicting annual expenditures. Call number sorts were used for collection maintenance and for faculty review. Other sorts, such as one by call number and then by publisher to demonstrate the most-important publishers by discipline were also possible.

Hamaker described the serials review project at Louisiana State University. Beginning one year before the review, the results of serials budget analysis were presented to the faculty senate and other campus groups. Faculty were asked to review the entire serials list which was arranged in call number order. They were asked to mark core titles "one"; needed titles "two"; and peripheral titles "three." The remainder of the titles, called "orphans," were not marked.

The fact that faculty reviewed the complete list, instead of only titles in their own discipline, proved to be important. Faculty marked many titles outside their own discipline, showing growing interdisciplinary research needs. Using the ratings provided by the faculty and data on use, librarians were able to choose titles to cancel. During this review project, only "orphans" had to be cancelled.

The workshop participants asked questions and offered comments throughout the presentation. The presenters used overheads and distributed a handout of twenty-four graphs and lists illustrating the points discussed during the session. Astle and Hamaker concluded that the data analysis conducted to date has been useful and that they are continuing to discover new publishing and pricing patterns, and their implications.

Automated Binding Control: Libraries, Binders and Serial Agents

Martin Gordon

Barry Baker, Technical Services, University of Georgia and Jack W. Tolbert, Vice-President, National Library Bindery, presented the results of two surveys conducted by Gary Pitkin (University of Northern Colorado), Doug Phelps (Vanderbilt University), and Baker. The surveys were designed to shed light upon the present relationships that are formed between the library, commercial binder and serial subscription agent as a result of the burgeoning use of various levels of automation.

In the fall of 1986, at the academic library section of the Faxon Users Group meeting in Boston, this question arose: Should computer-based serials control programs include a binding module capable of fulfilling all or part of the various traditional interfaces between academic libraries and binders? This question expressed an undercurrent of concern that had been heard by both binders and agents since 1981 when Faxon's SC-10 system was introduced. Should there be a generic model for such programs that could run in a variety of environments, or should the agent develop one system that would be functionally integrated at certain levels with the major library systems currently being marketed by vendors, or, perhaps, should the agent divorce itself entirely from this area of serials management support?

Faxon identified 120 current users of their automated serial control systems of whom one-third replied to a questionnaire. Compilation of this survey led to the mailing of a second questionnaire to thirty-eight commercial binders which yielded fourteen responses.

Martin Gordon, Periodicals/Microforms Librarian, Shadek-Fackenthal Library, Franklin & Marshall College, Lancaster, PA 17604.

Responding libraries differed greatly in their use of commercial bindery services. On the average, roughly $91,000 a year was expended on binding with approximately two-thirds of these funds spent on serials, the area in which the repetitive pattern of binding is most hospitable to applications of automated control. Despite this fact, libraries were evenly divided on the question of the importance of automated support provided by the binder as far as their selection of which binders to use. One respondent was simply not interested in use of computers in this area until "a machine was invented that would actually go to the shelf, collate the volume, and prepare it for binding!" Of those who did consider automated support in their decision making, ease of preparation and efficiencies that resulted in less preparation time were the leading motivations (factors which were later echoed in binders' responses.)

If automation was offered, the inclusion of fields for binding title(s), codes for covering material and color, special instructions, lettering foil colors, and call number/location data were most often cited as essential elements. The bindery ticket produced by the system should capture the above characteristics of each title as well as variable information for each physical volume along with special considerations such as the inclusion of separately published indices.

With regard to the responsibility for the initial inputing of binding data, nearly twice as many libraries felt that this was an area best performed by the binder, than libraries who felt that they themselves should initiate input. Sixteen percent saw this endeavor as a joint one.

Throughout the presentation's review of both surveys, audience interaction with the speakers provided helpful insights, especially those of Robert S. Coyle (Joseph Ruzicka-South) and Bruce F. Jacobsen (Bridgeport National Bindery). One point of lengthy discussion was the ethical implications of binder-supplied generic systems with regard to matters of data and applications programming ownership. Who owns which, and to what extent is the library "obliged" to remain with a binder if such a system is "given" to the library?

Nearly all libraries felt that the system should generate bindery tickets on a volume-by-volume basis and also expressed interest in systems that would advise the serials staff when physical units were ready for recall from the stacks (i.e., were complete and ready for binding).

Virtual unanimity was expressed by the commercial binders requiring the presence of automation in their work. Thirteen of the fourteen respondents stated that automation reduced costs, increased efficiency and minimized human error. In this vein, eleven binders offered some form of automated support to their customers with most systems functioning on the microcomputer level. While ten of these binders claimed to have certain points of interfacing with their own mainframe systems, none provided such links with serial agent control systems, at least at the time of the survey in early 1988.

As the survey of libraries revealed, so the binders survey agreed that quality of binding, product costs, turn-around time, and error rates were more important to libraries than the presence of automation. However, as competition among binders increases, value-added services such automated control of binding will place any one particular binder in a better marketing position.

In summary, then, it was apparent from both survey and audience responses that traditional gauges of commercial binding relationships will not be re-prioritized by technological innovations such as automation of processing and control. Nevertheless, use of automation with or without interfacing with serial subscription agent systems will be a widening avenue upon which both the library and the binder will proceed. Movement along this avenue will help insure the continuance of a growing sophistication in the academic library's pursuit of quality preservation of its print collections.

Automated Invoice Processing Using Vendor-Supplied Tapes

Joseph Raker

Two examples of the use of automated invoice processing were presented at this workshop. Diane McCutcheon, Serials Record Division, and Bill Willmering, Head-Serials Records Section, both of the National Library of Medicine (NLM), described their use of automated invoice processing using a system developed in-house. Roberta Corbin, Systems Analyst at the University of California, San Diego presented a similar process using INNOVACQ.

Although both systems were developed independently, the thought processes as well as the results were quite similar. Both libraries wanted to curtail the time needed for manual posting of invoices while maintaining the level of accuracy achieved in manual posting.

Willmering set the background for the need to automate the processing of invoices at NLM. Some 20,000 unique titles and 27,000 copies were actively received at NLM. About thirty postings per hour were done manually. This was both tedious and time-consuming, and resulted in staff being unable to keep abreast of claims or handle routine serial problems. Since check-in records on tape had been supplied by vendors for some years, it was hoped that invoice data on tapes could also be used. Consequently, the same vendors were asked to supply invoice data on tapes.

McCutcheon then outlined the Master Serials System (MSS) at NLM. This is a locally-developed serials system, in use for the past five years, which utilizes database management software called INQUIRE, a product of Infodata Inc. The MSS consists of a number

---

Joseph Raker, Acquisitions Librarian, Boston Public Library, 426 Pleasant Street, Apt. 21, Malden, MA 02148.

of files which are connected by a title control number. The three prime files are:

— the serials core file which contains bibliographic data;
— the SUBS file which contains subscription and invoice data;
— the CHECKIN file which contains current receipt and claims data.

Since 1983, invoice data has been added by means of vendor tapes. When these tapes are received at the library, an interim file must be created because no standardization of data is available. Consequently, pertinent information is parsed from the vendor tapes onto the interim file. Machine checks are then made to validate purchase order numbers, invoice numbers and procurement source. Validated invoices are added to the SUBS file and a proofing list of the invoice data is generated. This list, showing previous payments and title information, is verified against the original invoice. Once corrections have been made online, the data is loaded into the posting process. Invoices from sources not providing machine readable data, about 1/3 of NLM's subscriptions, are posted online.

Due to limitations of INQUIRE, only basic machine checks are made (invoice numbers and vendor names); hence, quality control is a major concern. However, five years experience in automated processing attest to the accuracy of the data transcriptions.

Willmering concluded the NLM presentation by expressing the hope that future enhancements might include more machine review of data. He would especially like to see a machine check of non-received or delayed titles.

At the University of California, San Diego, a similar approach was used. Corbin explained that in the Fall of 1987 implementation of the INNOVACQ System had already begun. The serials file, consisting of 20,000 active subscriptions and standing orders, had already been loaded with updated funds and vendor codes. In addition, six vendors have been given the tape specifications by INNOVACQ and five of the vendors have been Beta tested. The sixth vendor is currently being Beta tested.

Prior to the tape load, staff check paper copies of invoices for obvious problems. The tape is then loaded into a temporary storage disk (a 3M cassette) for processing. The system checks the validity of invoice information and purchase orders and then staff correct any invoice errors. Once the process is completed, the data is loaded into an accept/reject file where corrections to the order file are handled (funds, locations etc.). It is at this point that items may be removed from the invoice. Data is then accepted and processed into a pay file so that posting can be run. Processing of invoices from vendors not supplying machine-readable records is done on-line.

In concluding her presentation, Corbin cited several disadvantages of automated invoice processing:

- Of all the vendors who supplied tapes, only one vendor included titles. Others listed only purchase order numbers.
- Should the vendor bill for a title no longer on order, a dummy order must be created in order to move the data through the processing file into the accept/reject file where it can finally be rejected.
- Since processing notes are only found in the order records, staff must use a second terminal to check these notes when discrepancies are found in the invoice data.

Though automated invoice processing has some disadvantages, both presentations stressed the overall advantages of an automated system over manual posting. Automated invoice processing has saved valuable staff time and the accuracy of the posting records has been maintained.

The ensuing discussion period raised some informational questions from those attendees using automated invoice processing, especially those using INNOVACQ. Other substantive issues raised included: the perennial issue of standardization of machine readable records, quality control in accepting machine records, the reaction of auditors to electronic posting, reassignment of staff duties, and the need for communication between the subscription vendors and the vendors of automated systems.

Re-Automation of Serials Control: From OCLC's Serials Control Subsystem to INNOVACQ

Karen Sandlin Silverman

Kenneth L. Kirkland, Serials Librarian at DePaul University, presented an overview of DePaul's migration from OCLC's Serials Control Sybsystem to Innovative Interfaces' INNOVACQ. Anne S. Hudson, Associate Director of Systems and Access Services, helped prepare the paper and assisted with questions and discussion at the end of the presentation.

The General Libraries at DePaul implemented OCLC's Serials Control Subsystem in 1984. When OCLC announced the demise of the system, DePaul started planning for a replacement, a joint system between its general and law libraries. The first stage in this process was the identification of specifications the new system had to meet:

- Search capability from five sites
- Automated invoice processing
- Support processing capability (check-in, claiming, etc.) from three locations
- Compatibility with new acquisitions system to replace OCLC Acquisitions — also slated for deactivation
- Ability to generate local serials holdings list sorted by fund data.

The five systems reviewed were:

Karen Sandlin Silverman, Assistant Manager, OCLC Services Group, PALINET, 3401 Market Street, Suite 362, Philadelphia, PA 19104.

© 1988 by The Haworth Press, Inc. All rights reserved.

- SC350 — no remote access or processing supported;
- DOBIS/IBM — not readily available;
- URICA — not readily available and not in use in the U.S.;
- NOTIS — an integrated system and a strong contender but too expensive and its serials component too primitive;
- INNOVACQ — DePaul's ultimate choice in December 1986.

Kirkland then gave a brief overview of INNOVACQ's four kinds of records, bibliographic, order, check-in, and check-in cards. (The check-in cards could arguably be referred to as only half records since they are attached to check-in records.) During the initial conversion stages staff from DePaul made an invaluable contact with Winthrop College who also had converted from OCLC SCS to INNOVACQ. The Winthrop College staff gave much sound advice and sage warnings for DePaul as they prepared for implementation of INNOVACQ.

DePaul staff worked with Innovative Interfaces staff to prepare for implementation of INNOVACQ. Since their implementation style is "consultant-on-site" (and very effective), it seemed difficult to find out much before the tapeload. DePaul staff did study INNOVACQ's manual prior to implementation, but this did not prove to be very helpful. DePaul staff felt that a pre-installation questionnaire or profile might have made planning easier.

Kirkland next outlined the hardware and telecommunications issues. The DePaul set-up proved to be a bit of a challenge. One CPU had to serve three locations as well as printers, and a link with OCLC. Unfortunately, due to phone multiplexor limitations, some terminals must communicate at 1,200 baud as opposed to the 9,600 baud for the terminals directly cabled. There were a few initial problems with hardware, but all the problems seem to be resolved.

DePaul was then ready for the tapeload. OCLC had to provide two separate tapes: the General Libraries' tape with check-in data, and the Law Library's union list holdings tape. The Law Library had not been using the SCS check-in component.

INNOVACQ's trainer arrived during the week of 11 May 1987. Initial training gave more emphasis to the acquisitions component of the system, although DePaul had slated Serials as its first priority. Nonetheless, the five days of intensive training with various groups of staff proceeded smoothly and were very effective.

During a three week period when the OCLC system was unavailable and the tapeload conversion had not taken place, DePaul, in order to avoid a backlog keyed records into INNOVACQ for all items received in the day's mail.

Soon after the tapeload had been completed eight problem areas surfaced. These included: having to insert spaces after the "PER." (call number prefix) in 5,198 records; merging 756 records keyed in manually; deleting unwanted 082 fields; constructing 46 check-in records; reconstructing holdings where volume equalled a year; and editing holding library codes. Two other more serious problems led to the re-loading of almost 2,000 records. Approximately 1,700 records had to be retapeloaded due to damage or truncation during conversion, and 256 records that were bumped at the time of tapeload because Innovative Interfaces assumed DePaul had not exceeded 500 records during manual processing had to be re-downloaded. Numbering began with "500" when in fact DePaul had keyed 756 records.

Kirkland next outlined three large projects to be undertaken. The first project, automated invoice posting, has been successfully implemented for both Faxon and Blackwell. As Kirkland describes it, this is one of the major benefits of "INNOVACQuation." The next step will be to go online with vendors. The second big project was to identify and edit approximately 800 current subscription records not previously activated. Kirkland refers to the last project as "longer-range edits." Fund codes were added to all live check-in records (the next stage will be to include dead titles) to accommodate DePaul's local practice of printing serials holdings lists sorted on fund codes. All microform records are to be edited to add location and identity codes for specific microformat (i.e., microfilm, microopaque, microfiche). The last of these longer range edits will be the deletion in dead records of unnecessary fields left over from OCLC.

Kirkland concluded with some "after-the-fact realizations" and "dilemmas." (1) An additional 5,000 more check-in records than originally planned had to be purchased. This came about because of failure to comprehend fully that even dead records would require check-in records to accommodate the LDR fields from the tapeload. (Libraries must purchase records in blocks of 10,000 with upper limits set by disk space.) (2) DePaul gradually realized that it would be easier to coordinate duplicate titles between the Law and General Libraries with duplicate bibliographic records. (The General Libraries use DDC and the Law Library uses LC classification.) (3) For some reason the FUND and DTRD (date received) fields were not downloaded from the OCLC records. (4) There were errors with receiving location codes which were easy to identify and fix. (5) DePaul developed its own claiming profile for shelf-checking before printing claims. (6) DePaul is happy with INNOVACQ's claiming functions, even though some local procedures have circumvented the system as set up. (7) The bindery component was implemented late — it could not handle DDC easily until Release 7 which was installed in March 1988. (8) The paper serials holdings list is still being generated from OCLC union list tapes. (9) INNOVACQ options for printing holdings lists are costly either in time or money. (10) DePaul is still wrestling with the way to handle holdings statements so as to make them understandable yet not take up too much computer storage space.

The formal presentation ended on an upbeat note — overall DePaul is quite pleased with INNOVACQ. During the discussion period, participants had an opportunity to discuss in more detail areas of concern such as downloading, system response time, vendor response to problems, staff morale, public access to the system, the purchase of new equipment, the apparent lack of communication between OCLC and Innovative Interfaces.

This dialogue, as good dialogue should, gave both presenters and audience an opportunity to interact on many levels and in many ways which will aid them in the months and years to come.

Is There Life After Serials?

Eleanor I. Cook

This workshop, moderated by N. Bernard "Buzzy" Basch, was intended to give attendees tips on how to use their serials experience to further professional goals. The panelists, all of whom had worked with serials at some point in their careers, shared their personal stories about how serials work had aided them in their advancement.

The first speaker was Judy McQueen, presently Senior Consultant for Information Consultants, Inc. Having started her career in serials cataloging McQueen became heavily involved in serials automation in Australia and eventually became Principal Librarian at the National Library of Australia. After a brief stint as a representative at the Australian Embassy in the U.S., her career reached a turning point. She assessed her background and concluded that with the amount of automation experience she had, it would be possible to go into consulting. McQueen did consulting for a period of time, became Vice President of a private company for a while, and then went back into consulting.

McQueen began her presentation by asking each person in the room to state his or her current position and to give a brief statement on future career goals. She then used this information to illustrate some of the positive qualities serials work can bring to job development. Her message to the audience was that serials experience can be successfully transferred outside of the library world if one can learn to translate those skills to a broader context. McQueen went on to explain that it is particularly important to get past library jar-

---

Eleanor I. Cook, Serials Catalog Librarian and Supervisor in the Serials Department, North Carolina State University Libraries, Box 7111, North Carolina State University, Raleigh, NC 27695-7111.

© 1988 by The Haworth Press, Inc. All rights reserved.

gon. Many examples, primarily in the form of action verbs such as one might find on a resumé or in a job description, were given. For example instead of referring to "Kardex check-in," using the phrase "inventory control" may facilitate successful job placement outside of a traditional library setting. In addition McQueen suggested use of terms such as "budget allocating," "service assessment," and "procedure development," which can be readily understood in various business settings.

The second speaker was Helen Citron Wiltse. Wiltse, who is presently Associate Director, Georgia Institute of Technology Libraries, began her career at Georgia Tech as Gifts and Exchange Librarian. In that position, and in others along the way, she worked extensively with serials and the problems inherent with them. In her presentation Wiltse said that she felt that serials work was excellent preparation for future administrators. She then pointed out that three of the six administrators at the Georgia Tech Libraries have a serials background. In addition, Wiltse pointed out that many of the qualities needed when working with serials were also the qualities looked for when persuing an administrative post. Among those shared qualities are the ability to:

— be flexible and to be able to handle rapid change;
— be responsible and to pay attention to detail;
— be able to manage people and resources;
— have good problem solving skills;
— have had exposure to the challenge of automating serials, the most complex part of any library system.

Wiltse, who now devotes a large part of her time to negotiating contracts with online database vendors, credits her past experiences with serial vendors with aiding her in her present duties. She concluded with the comment that for her, it was not a question of "Is there life after serials?" but rather, "Is there life without serials?"

The third speaker was Ann L. Okerson, Manager of Library Services for Jerry Alper, Inc. Okerson spoke of her experiences in the private sector and how she arrived there after years of academic library work.

Okerson worked her way up the ranks in a medium-sized academic library in British Columbia where much of her work was concentrated in serials. Feeling a need for something different, Okerson found the business side of library services to be attractive. Consequently she obtained a position with a small company, Jerry Alper, Inc., that buys and sells backfiles and retrospective collections of serials. Since most of her customers are academic libraries, Okerson's experience in the academic setting has proved invaluable in understanding her customers' needs.

Okerson then went on to compare and contrast working in an academic setting with working in the private sector. Working for a private company is different from working in an academic library because:

- There is a greater amount of personal risk involved — the profitability of a company is often directly related to employee performance;
- Due to the fast pace, there are fewer chances for normal social contacts;
- It is harder to keep up with professional developments;
- One must be self-motivated, self-disciplined, flexible, and have good health and stamina;
- One must be personable with clients but also crisp and to the point;
- One must be independent — often there is no one to back you up if you have a family emergency or are ill;
- It is possible to have a higher salary, but one must work for it (that is, it does not happen quickly).

In contrast the academic world tends to operate at a slower pace but usually offers good benefits.

In closing Okerson observed that librarians sometimes express the concern that if they decide they like an academic environment better than the private sector, they are not able to return to academe easily. She said that this is not necessarily true. People with broad experience find that they receive offers from a variety of organizations. "The more you do, the more you *can* do," she remarked.

Rebecca T. Lenzini started out doing serials check-in and claiming in a large academic library, and progressed through the system by tackling "massive, wretched projects" (such as retrospective conversion) with a "smiling, can-do attitude." This, she stated, is a quality which administrators welcome and which can help move one up the ladder. For Lenzini, "one great project led to another." In short, she found that taking on impossible tasks and actually completing them gives one greater chances for promotion as well as more speaking and writing opportunities.

In 1981 when she joined The Faxon Company, Lenzini discovered that serials are a mystery to most people. Having the ability to explain this mystery in a non-threatening manner helped to educate and reduce the anxiety in people who did not understand serials but found it necessary to do so. (In recent years, vendors have made an effort to hire librarians for this very reason.) Also, Lenzini suggested that becoming involved in new technologies and the financial management of an organization helps a person to find new avenues to career possibilities.

Buzzy Basch ended the session with some summary comments followed by a short question and answer period. In his comments Basch mentioned that opportunities are out there for anyone willing to go after them. If one is "willing to do windows" at the outset, growth is possible. He noted that there are many job openings presently in the library profession and related areas.

During the question and answer period, two of the questions posed were: How does one deal with marriage and children when travelling in a high pressure private sector position, and how can serial catalogers break out of their ruts? In answer to the latter, the panel itself illustrated that serials cataloging can lead to many possibilities. They urged the audience not to be afraid to go out and apply for positions that might be a little different from what they are used to. The answer to the former, however, was not quite so clear cut. The panelists agreed that this is a tough issue for many people, but particularly for women. Non-traditional arrangements such as having househusbands, commuter marriages, or nannys seem to work for some couples. However, a more traditional job setting or part-time work may be more suitable for people raising a family. Creative job arrangements are becoming more common, so there are ways to have a career and children too.

North American Serials Interest Group Third Annual Conference — Oglethorpe University, June 1988

Conference Registrants	Institution
Ahtola, Anneli	University of Colorado at Denver
Aiello, Helen	Westleyan University
Alexander, James	Cambridge University Press
Anderson, Greg	University of Georgia Libraries
Anderson, Jan	Utah State University
Anderson, Marcia	Arizona State University
Astle, Deana	Clemson University
Aufdemberge, Karen	University of Toledo
Ayres, Leighann	
Bailey, Dorothy	Georgia Institute of Technology
Baker, Carol	Canada Institute of Scientific and Technical Information
Baldwin, Jane	
Banach, Patricia	University of Massachusetts
Barnes, Roy	University of Toledo
Barry, Jane	Nassau Community College
Basch, Bernard	Turner Subscriptions
Basler, Annette	Cardinal Stritch College Library
Beerman, Sandy	Bowling Green State University
Bergholz, Donna	Duke University
Bevis, Mary	Houston Cole Library
Boggan, Dee	Medical University of South Carolina
Braden Jr., Jim	Georgia State University/College of Law
Breedlove, Rebecca	University of Mass/Boston
Breton, Gabriel	National Library of Canada
Broadway, Rita	Memphis State University
Bross, Valerie	Cal Polytecnic
Brown-May, Patricia	University of Michigan/Dearborn
Bushell, Christiane	Michigan State University
Bustion, Marifran	Texas A & M University
Butler, Beverley	

Callahan, Patricia — University of Pennsylvania
Cap, Maria — University of Southern California
Carlson, Barbara — Medical University of South Carolina

Carrington, Bradley — Northwestern University Library
Casto, Lisa — University of South Florida Library/Serials Dept.

Catau, Jennine — Bowling Green State University
Chadwick, Leroy — University of Washington
Champagne, Thomas — Northwestern University Library
Chang, Chia/Ching — Bucknell University
Chao, Theresa — University of Wisconsin
Chatterton, Leigh
Christ, Ruth — University of Iowa
Churukian, Araxie — University of California
Clack, Mary — Harvard College Library
Clay, Genevieve — Eastern Kentucky University
Cline, Sharon — EBSCO Subscription Services
Connell, Tschera — University of Illinois/Graduate School of Library and Information

Cook, Eleanor — North Carolina State University
Corbin, Roberta — University of Cal/San Diego
Courtney, Keith — Taylor and Francis Ltd.
Czech, Isabel — Institute for Scientific Information
Davis, Susan — State University of New York at Buffalo

Deeken, JoAnne — James Madison University
Degner, Christie — University of North Carolina/Chapel Hill

Devin, Robin — University of Rhode Island
Durden, Iris — Georgia Southern College
Early, Caroline — National Agricultural Library
Echt, Rita — Michigan State University
Edelman, Marla
Elder, Nelda — Kansas State University
Elswick, Rebecca — Mary Washington College
Etkin, Cynthia — Eastern Kentucky University
Farmer, Diana — Farrell Library
Feick, Tina — Blackwell's Periodicals
Feldman, Immie — University of Pennsylvania
Finlay, Alison — University of New Hampshire
Finn, Meg
Foggin, Carol — University of Tennessee
Folsom, Sandy — Central Michigan University
Foster, Constance — Western Kentucky University

Fugle, Mary	Springer-Verlag New York Inc.
Fulton, Bruce	Mercy College
Gartrell, Joyce	Columbia University
Gelenter, Win	National Agricultural Library
Geller, Marilyn	Massachusetts/Institute of Technology Libraries
Gillespie, E.	University of Kansas Libraries
Gilmore, Peggy	Georgia Southern College
Glasgow, Kay	SUNY Binghamton
Goetham, Jeri	Duke University
Goldstein, Rosalyn	Widener University
Gordon, Martin	Franklin and Marshall College
Gormley, Alice	Memorial Library
Gorsuch, Chris	Clemson University
Hajdas, Susan	Princeton University Library
Hanson, Martha	Syracuse University
Harber, Patty	Mercer University
Hardy, Lenore	Medical College of Pennsylvania
Harman, Amanda	University of NC Charlotte
Hart, Eileen	Berea College
Hartman, Anne-Marie	Queens College Library
Hayman, Lynne	EBSCO
Hayman, Lynne	EBSCO Subscription Service
Helms, Mary	Washington University/School of Medicine
Hepfer, Cindy	State University New York/Buffalo
Heroux, Marlene	EBSCO Subscription Services
Hill, Sherry	
Holley, Beth	University of Alabama
Hollyfield, Diane	George Washington University
Houbeck Jr., Robert	University of Michigan Library
Hsu, Karen	New York Public Library
Hsueh, Daphne	Ohio State University
Huff, Susan	Franklin and Marshall College Library
Irvin, Judy	Louisiana Technical University
Ivins, October	National Institute for Environmental Health Sciences
Jaeger, Don	Alfred Jaeger Inc.
Jaeger, Glenn	Alfred Jaeger Inc.
Jager, Con	Martinus Nijhoff International
Jenson, Norma	College of Charleston
Johnson, David	Princeton University
Johnson, Jane	Georgia Southern College
Johnson, Judy	University of Nebraska/Lincoln

Jones, David	University of Alberta
Keating II, Lawrence	University of Houston Libraries
Kellogg, Martha	
Kelly, Margaret	Bloomsburg University
Kennedy, Kit	Coutts Library Services
Kersey, Harriet	
Ketcham, Lee	EBSCO Industries Inc.
Kie, Kathleen	
Kirby, Shirley	Swarthmore College Library
Kirkland, Kenneth	DePaul University
Knupp, Blaine	Indiana University of PA
Krissiep, Margot	Washington State University
Kropf, Blythe	New York Public Library
Lane, Alice	University of Nebraska-Lincoln
Lange, Janice	Sam Houston State University
Leachman, Charles	EBSCO Subscription Services
Leazer, William	Majors Scientific Books
Lenzini, Rebecca	CARL Systems Inc.
Levin, Fran	Houston Public Library
Lewis, Diane	U.S. Geological Survey Library
Lindsay, Robin	University of South Carolina/Columbia
Linke, Erika	Carnegie Mellon University
Lonberger, Jana	Georgia Institute of Technology
Long, Maurice	British Medical Association
Luckett, Lynne	
Luke, Joan	Georgia State University
Lupone, George	Cleveland State University
Luther, Judy	FAXON
Lynden, Frederick	Brown University
MacAdam, Carol	Princeton University
Madden, Maureen	Pergamon Journals Inc.
Maddox, Jane	
Magenau, Carol	University of Connecticut
Malinowski, Teresa	California State University Fullerton
Mann, Caroline	Houston Academy of Medicine
Markley, Susan	Villanova University
Markwith, Michael	FAXON
Marshall, Graham	Butterworth Legal Publishers
Martin, Sylvia	Vanderbilt University
May, Charlea	Birmingham Public Library
Mazuk, Melody	Southern Baptist Theo Seminar
McAdam, Tim	Appalachian State University
McArtor, Kathryn	Denison University
McBride, Donna	Boston Public Library

McCann, Jett	Medical College of Georgia
McCann, Kristine	McGregor Subscription Service
McCarter, Bobbye	Georgia Southwestern College
McConnell, Christopher	Simmons College/Graduate School of Library and Information
McCutcheon, Dianne	National Library of Medicine
McDonough, Joyce	Ekstrom Library/University of Louisville
McIver, Carol	Princeton University
McKenney, Nancy	Eastern Kentucky University
McLaren, Mary	University of Kentucky
McRae, Barry	Columbia University
McReynolds, Rosalee	Loyola University
Meiseles, Linda	Brooklyn College
Memmott, Kirk	Bringham Young University
Meneely, Kathleen	Case Western Reserve University
Merriman, John	B. H. Blackwell
Merryman, Peggy	US Geological Survey Library
Mershon, Loretta	North Carolina State University
Mesner, Lillian	University of Kentucky Agriculture Library
Meyle, Joyce	AMOCO Corporation
Miller, Daphne	Wright State University/Fordham Health Sciences Library
Moles, Jean	University of Arkansas for Medical Science
Narayanan, Kamala	Queens University
Nason, Stanley	Read-More Publications Inc.
Okerson, Ann	Jerry Alper Inc.
O'Neil, Rosanna	Marketing and User Services Division
Orser, Frank	University of Florida
Patrick, Carol	Cleveland State University
Paulk, Betty	Valdosta State College
Penick, Patricia	IEEE
Phillips, Sharon	Cal State University Hayward
Piesbergen, Frances	University of Missouri
Pittman, Pam	Western Carolina University
Postlethwaite, Bonnie	Linx Services
Presley, Roger	William Russell Pullen Library
Radencich, John	Florida International University
Raines, M.	State Library of North Dakota
Raker, Joseph	Boston Public Library
Ralston, Joan	Villanova Universtiy
Rast, Elaine	Northern Illinois University

Reed, Virginia	Northwestern Illinois University
Reich, Victoria	Stanford University
Rice, Patricia	The Pennsylvania State University
Riddick, John	Central Michigan University
Rieke, Judith	Vanderbilt University
Roberts, Elizabeth	Owen S/E Library
Robischon, Rose	United States Military Academy
Robnett, Bill	Rice University Library
Rogers, Nancy	EBSCO Subscription Services
Rossignol, Lucien	Smithsonian Institution Libraries
Russell, Carrie	University of Arizona
Saxe, Minna	Grad School Library
Sayler, Terry	University of Maryland
Scanland, Roger	University of Arizona
Scanlon, Brian	Elsevier Science Publishing Co Inc.
Schwartz, Marla	Washington College of Law Library/American University
Schwartzkopf, Rebecca	Mankato State University
Sciplin, Marlene	AMOCO Corporation
Scott, Sharon	University of Arizona
Scullin, Jan	Massachusetts General Hospital
Sexton, Ebba	University of Kentucky/Law Library
Shelock, E.	Royal Society of Chemistry
Shelton, Judith	Georgia Institute of Technology
Sheppard, Jan	Solinet
Silverman, Karen	Palinet
Sleep, Esther	Brock University
Smith, Dorcas	University of Houston Libraries
Smith, Susan	University of Connecticut
Smith, Susan	West Georgia College
Soderholm, Dorothy	University of Nebraska
Soper, Mary	University of Washington
Spell, Cynthia	University of Massachusetts
Stapleton, Diana	Eastern Kentucky University
Steele, Heather	Blackwell's Periodical Division
Stevens, Lisa	University of California
Strauch, Katina	College of Charleston Library
Sullivan, Eugene	University of South Alabama
Sutherland, Carol	Library of Parliament
Tagler, John	Elsevier Science
Talley, Kaye	University of Central Arkansas
Tallman, Karen	University of Arizona
Tenney, Joyce	UMBC Albin O Kuhn Library
Terry, Nancy	Grand Valley State College
Thomas, Nancy	Ohio State University

Thompson, J.	Scholarly Book Center
Thomson, Sarah	
Thornberry, Patricia	University of South Florida
Thorne, Kathleen	San Jose State University
Tiffany, William	Memorial University of Newfoundland
Timberland, Phoebe	University of New Orleans
Tolbert, Jack	National Library Bindery Co.
Topfer, Sue	Wilkes College
Tracy, Joan	Eastern Washington University
Tribit, Donald	Millersville University
Turitz, Mitch	
Tuttle, Marcia	University of NC/Chapel Hill
Upham, Lois	University of South Carolina
Vent, Marilyn	University of Nevada
Vidor, Ann	Georgia Institute of Technology
Visk, Linda	Emory University
Wachel, Kathy	University of Iowa Libraries
Waite, Marjory	University of North Carolina
Walker, Elaine	Cornell University Libraries
Wallace, Patricia	University of Northern Colorado
Wang, Anna	Ohio State University Libraries
Ward, Jeannette	University Central Florida Libraries
Warren, Karen	University of South Carolina
Welch, Mary	University of Kentucky
Weng, Cathy	Tufts University
Wharton, Patrick	D Reidel Publishing Company
Wilcox, Donald	University of Michigan
Wilhelme, Judy	University of Michigan
Wilhite, Marjorie	University of Iowa Libraries
Wilkas, Lenore	University of Pennsylvania
Williams, Geraldine	Northern Kentucky University
Williams, Susan	University of Colorado
Williamson, Marilyn	Georgia Institute of Technology
Willmering, Bill	National Library of Medicine
Wilson, Betty	Morehead State University
Winchester, David	Washburn University
Wirtz, Theresa	Yankee Book Peddler
Wood, Don	Southern Illinois University
Woods, Gale	Winthrop College
Youles, Kathryn	Dalton College
Youmans, Mary	Western Carolina University

Index

AACR 1,133
AACR 2,100,109,114,133-134,135,138
ADONIS, 85-91
    CD-ROM storage and, 85,86,88-89,
        90-91,96,97
    collection, 88-89
    document preparation, 87
    Information on Demand and, 88,89-90
    serial article identifier, 93,94,96-98
    technical aspects, 87-88
Agreement on Guidelines for Classroom Copying in Not-For Profit Educational Institutes, 63
American Library Association (ALA)
    Association of College and Research Libraries, 109
    MARBI Committee, 109,135
American National Standard (ANSI), 95,96
American Society of Composers, Authors, and Performers (ASCAP), 69
Anderson, Greg, 145,146
AppleCD SC CD-ROM drive, 124-125
Archives, photocopying by, 34-36,64-65
Article identifier, 93-98
ASCII, 58,105
Association of College and Research Libraries, 109
Association of American Publishers (AAP), 59-60,61-62
Astle, Dean, 153-154,155
Author, as copyright owner, 57

Baker, Barry, 157
Basch, N. Bernard, 169,172
BIBLID, 93,94,95-96
Bibliographic control, of serials, 133-139
    CONSER and, 134-135,136,137,138
    foreign records, 134-135

International Serials Data system, 138
    multiple versions, 135,136-137
Bibliographic Input Standards, 104
Billington, James, 61
Binding control, automated, 157-159
Blackwell Scientific Publications, Ltd, 88, 167
Book(s)
    Copyright Clearance Center registration, 50,51
    discount, 128
    pricing of, 118,121-122
        booksellers' operating cost and, 128
        production cost and, 119,121-122
        promotion cost and, 122-123
        vendors' service charges and, 120
Book Industry Study Group, 95
Bookseller, operating costs, 128
British Library Document Service Centre, Document Supply Centre, 59-60,88, 97
British Library Lending Division, 85
BRS, 100
BRS After Dark, 78
Budget
    analysis, 153-155
    percentage for serials, 150
Butterworth Scientific Publishers, 1-2,88. *See also* IPC Science and Technology Press
    new journal development process, 3-22

Cambridge University Press, 143
Cameron, Jamie, 97
Campbell, Robert, 22
Canada, electronic journal access in, 73-83
CANMARC, 134

Cardinal Industries, Inc. v. *Anderson Parrish Associates, Inc.*, 70n.
Cataloging, of computer files, 99-116
  guidelines, 109
  variant titles, 104,106-108
Catalog records, retrospective conversion, 81,137
CD/International, 105
CD-ROM
  ADONIS and, 85,86,88-89,90-91,96,97
  copyright implications, 62
  cost, 75
  databases, cataloging of, 99-116
  end-user searches, 78
  future of, 90-91
  licensing fee, 75
  microforms versus, 105
  online access versus, 74-76,78,79-80,83
Centre Francais du Copyright, 52
Check-in record, 166,167-168
Churchill Livingstone, 88
Clapper, Mary Ellen, 97
Clemson University Library, 153-155
Community College Association for Instruction and Technology, 109
Compact Disclosure, 78,83,105
Composites, 4,6
Computer file, cataloging of, 99-116
  guidelines, 109
  variant titles, 104,106-108
CONSER, 134-135,136,138
  Linked Systems Project, 135,136
  non-OCLC libraries, 136
  U.S. Newspaper Project, 137
CONTU, 30,33,37
Copyright, 23-40
  abuses of, 58-60
  CD-ROM publishing and, 62
  Congress and, 27,29,30-31,34
  CONTU guidelines, 30,33,37
  "fair use" concept, 63
  direct use, 28
  educational-related photocopying, 36-37, 57-58,63-71
  industrial libraries and, 30-32
  interlibrary loan and, 30,33,38
  librarians' interpretation of, 29-30,37
  library associations and, 29-30,37
  multiple copies and, 31,32-33,57-58, 63-71
  royalty fees, 32
  single-copy provision, 28,29,30-32, 34-36,38
  technology and, 39
Copyright Agency Limited, 52
Copyright Clearance Center, 43-54
  Annual Authorization Service, 44-46,48, 49,52,60
  article identifier number, 96
  Business Development Department, 53
  education-related photocopying and, 69
  establishment of, 32,43
  Foreign Authorization Program, 52
  Institute of Electrical and Electronics Engineers and, 57,60
  library associations and, 32
  new markets, 53-54
  publisher/title registrations, 50-51
  Reproduction Rights Organizations and, 43,52-53
  royalty fees, 44-49,51-52,53
  site licensing by, 44-46,48-49
    corporations, 43,44-46,48,49,53
    licensing fees, 33,48
    number of sites, 24,46,48-49
    university libraries, 23,53-54,69
  titles registered with, 24
  Transactional Reporting Service, 44, 46-48,51,52
Copyright infringement suits, 37,58-59, 66-67,70n.
Copyright Law of 1976, 23,57
  Congress and, 27,30-31,64
  copyright ownership and, 64-65
  criteria, 66
  multiple copies provision, 31,32-33, 57-58,63-71
  purpose, 64
  Section 107, 36-37,65-69
    "fair use" concept, 30,31,32,33, 65-69
  Section 108(g), 30,31,32,33,39,64-65
    See also Copyright Law of 1976, single-copy provision
  single-copy provision, 27,28,29,30-32, 38

violations, 64
Copyright Licensing Agency, 52
Copy shops, 59,60-61
Corporate libraries
   Copyright Clearance Center license, 43, 44-46,48,49
   copyright infringement suits against, 59
Coyle, Robert S., 158
Curtis, Mary E., 95
C.V. Mosby Company, 88

Database. *See also* names of specific databases
   on CD-ROM, cataloging of, 99-116
   online. *See also* names of specific databases
   number of, 79
Datext, 105
Dawson, 12
DePaul University Library, 165-169
DIALOG, 100
Digital Video Interactive, 89
Directory of Online Databases, 79
Directory of Periodicals Online, 73,79
DISCLOSURE, 78,83,105
DOBIS/IBM, 166
DOCMATCH, 98
Dutton, Stella, 4

Ehmard, John Paul, 73
Elsevier Science Publishing, 88,142-143
Enzyme and Microbial Technology, 4,6
ERIC, 79,83
EURONET DIANNE, 96
Exchange rate, journal prices and, 141-143

Faxon, 95,154-155,167
   SC-10 system, 149,157
   Users Group, 157
Ford, Gerald, 66
Futato, Linda, 73

Georg Thieme Verlag, 88
Guidelines for Using AACR2 Chapter 9 for Cataloging Microcomputer Software, 109
Guide to CD-ROMs in Print, 80

Hamaker, Charles, 153-154,155
Harper and Row Publishers, Inc. v. Nation Enterprises, 66-67
Hendley, Tom, 105
Holdings
   INNOVACQ and, 168
   USMARC Format, 145-147
Hudson, Anne S., 165

ILLINET ONLINE, 151
Industrial libraries. *See also* Corporate libraries
   photocopying by, 30-32
Information on Demand, 88,89-90
INFOTRAC, 83
INNOVACQ, 161,162-163
   re-automation with, 165-169
Innovative Interfaces, 166,168
INQUIRE, 161,162
Institute of Electrical and Electronics Engineers (IEEE), copyright policy, 55-62
Inter, Sheila S., 109
Interlibrary loan, photocopying guidelines and, 30,33
International Federation of Reproduction Rights Organizations, 53,60
International Organization for Standardization (ISO), 93,94
International Serials Data System (ISDS), 138
International Standard Serial Number (ISSN), 95,96,138,139n.
Invoice
   automated posting, 161-163,167
   without purchase order, 149
IPC Science and Technology Press, 3-4,7, 18
ISBD, 133
ISDS, 138
ISO, 93,94
ISSN, 95,96,138,139n.

Jacobsen, Bruce F., 158
Jager, Con, 141-142
Johnson v. *University of Virginia*, 70
John Wiley & Sons, Ltd., 88
Journal(s). *See also* Serial(s); names of specific journals
  economics of publishing, 1-22
    new journal development, 3-22
  electronic
    accessing, 73-83
    CD-ROM versus, 74-76,78,79-80,83
    definition, 74
  foreign, pricing, 141-143,153-154
  handling charges, 119-120
  new
    development process, 3-22
    pricing, 8,10,11,12,15,17-19
  pricing, 117-131,153-155
    discounts, 143
    discrimination in, 153-154
    exchange rates and, 141-143
    factors affecting, 118-120,121-122, 123,142
    of foreign journals, 141-143,153-154
    of new journals, 8,10,11,12,15,17-19
    photocopying and, 23
    vendor/librarian/publisher relationship and, 125,126,127,128-129,130-131
    vendors' service charges, 119-120, 126-127
    vendors and, 124-130
  production cost, 119
  promotion cost, 12,17,20,123
  refereeing of, 24
Journal of the American Medical Association, 91
Journal articles
  photocopying of. *See* Photocopying
  identifiers, 93-98
Journal Publishing (Page, Campbell and Meadows), 22

Karger, 143
Karolinska Institute, 88
Kinokuniya, 88
Kirkland, Kenneth L., 165,166,167
Komorous, Hana, 74
Kopinor, 52

Ladd, David, 36,65
Lancet, 91
Lenzini, Rebecca T., 171-172
LIAS, 149-150
Librarian. *See also* Serials librarian
  vendor/publisher relationship, 125,126, 127,128-129,130-131
Library associations. *See also* names of specific library associations
  copyright and, 29-30,37
  Copyright Clearance Center and, 32
Library of Congress
  NACO authority file, 136
  optical disk project, 61
Library Information Access System (LIAS), 149-150
Library technical assistant, 150-151
Lieb, Charles, 31-32
Linked Systems Project, 135,136
LITA, 109
Literar-Mechana, 52
Location, USMARC Format for, 145-147
Louisiana State University Library, serials budget analysis, 153-155

Machine-Readable Data Files Format, 100
Machine-Readable Form of Bibliographic Information (MARBI), 109,135
MARC records, 109
  CANMARC, 134
  international exchange of, 134
  UKMARC, 134
  USMARC, 109,135,137
    format for Holdings and Locations, 145-147
Marcus v. *Rowley*, 67
Master Serials System (MSS), 161-162
McCutcheon, Diane, 161
McQueen, Judy, 169-170
Meadows, Jack, 22
Microcomputer, automated binding control with, 157-159
Microcomputer file, cataloging of, 99-116
  guidelines, 109
  variant titles, 104,106-108
Microform, CD-ROM versus, 105
Monograph. *See also* Book(s)

Copyright Clearance Center registration, 50
Mosby, C.V., 88
Multiple copies, 31,32-33,36-37,57-58, 63-71
Multiple versions, 135,136-137
Munksgaard International Publishers Ltd., 88

NACO, 136
National Commission on New Technological Uses of Copyrighted Works (CONTU), 30,33,37
National Information Standards Organization (NISO), 93,94,109
National Library of Medicine, 161-162
New England Journal of Medicine, 91
Newsletter, full-text online, 77
Newspaper
  full-text online, 77
  U.S. Newspaper Project, 137
New York University, copyright infringement suit, 37,59,67
NISO, 93,94,109
Northern Illinois University Library, 150-151
NOTIS, 166
NTIS, 79

OCLC, 136
  Cataloging Subsystem, 99,100,101-103
  database size, 81
  machine-readable data file (MRDF) records, 99,100
  Serials Control Subsystem, re-automation and, 165-169
Ohio State University Libraries, 100,104
Okerson, Ann L., 170-171
On Acquisition (Melcher), 126
Online searching, full-text. *See also* Journal, electronic
  CD-ROM versus, 74-76,78,79-80,83
  end-user search, 78
Optical disk project, 61
Optical technology, 109. *See also* CD-ROM

Page, Gillian, 22,97
Paul, Sandra S., 97
Pennsylvania State University Library, 149-151
Pergamon Journals, 88
Phelps, Doug, 157
Photocopy
  direct use of, 28
  as journal subscription substitute, 32
Photocopying. *See also* Copyright
  of IEEE-published material, 57-58
  journal price effects, 23
  multiple copies, 31,32-33,36-37,57-58, 63-71
    Copyright Clearance Center and, 69
    copyright owners' permission for, 67-68
    for educational purposes, 36-37,57-58, 63-71
    "fair use" concept and, 65-69
    for library reserve, 65
    royalty fees and, 44-45,68
  for preservation, 65
  of software, 53,54
Pilkin, Gary, 157
Polymer, 4,5,6
Pooley, Christopher, 73-74
Prolitteris-Teledrama, 52
Public libraries, Copyright Clearance Center and, 49
Public Services, Technical Services cooperation with, 149-151
Publisher. *See also* specific publishers
  Copyright Clearance Center and, 44-49, 50-51
    copying fee, 44-49,50-51
    ISBN prefix, 50-51
    royalty distributions, 51-52
    title registrations, 50-51
  copyright ownership by, 23,57
  electronic. *See also* Journal(s), electronic
    return policy, 99-100
  foreign, 153-154. *See also* Journal, foreign
  journal pricing by. *See* Journal(s), pricing of
  librarian/vendor relationship, 125,126, 127,128-129,130-131
  refereeing by, 24

RASD, 109
Rast, Elaine, 150-151
Rawlin, Chris, 4
Reed International, 2
Refereeing, of scientific journals, 24
Reference book, full-text online, 77
Reference questions, serials-related, 150
Register of Copyrights, 34-36,39,65
Reproduction rights. *See also* Photocopying
  under Copyright Law of 1976, 64-65
Reproduction Rights Organizations (RRO), 43,52-53,60
Retrospective conversion, 81,137
Rice, Patricia Ohl, 149-150
Richard Anderson Photography v. *Radford University*, 70
RLIN, 81,136
Romaniuk, Elena, 74
Rowe, Richard, 95
Royalty fee, for photocopying, 32,44-49, 51,52,53,68
RTSD, 109
Russon, David, 97

SAID, 93,94,95-96,97-98
SC10, 149,157
SC350, 166
Serial(s). *See also* Journal(s)
  article identifiers, 93-98
  bibliographic control, 133-139
    CONSER and, 134-135,136,137,138
    foreign records, 134-135
    International Serials Data System, 138
    multiple versions, 135,136-137
  budget, 150
    analysis, 153-155
  Copyright Clearance Center registration, 50,51
  microcomputer file cataloging of, 99-116
  reference questions related to, 150
  Technical Services/Public Services cooperation regarding, 149-151
  unsolicited receipts for, 149-151
Serial Issue and Article Identifier (SAID), 93,94,95-96,97-98
Serials agent. *See also* Vendor as library's advocate, 128
Serials control
  binding module, 157-159
  re-automation of, 165-168
Serials Industry Systems Advisory Committee (SISAC), 93,94,95,97, 98
Serials librarian, career development, 169-172
Serials manager, 127,128,129. *See also* Serial librarian
SilverPlatter, 100
SISAC, 93,94,95,97,98
Software
  for computer file cataloging, 104
  as multiple version, 136
  photocopying of, 53,54
Sony Corporation of America v. *Universal Cities Studio*, 66
Springer-Verlag GmbH, 88
States, copyright infringement suits against, 70n.
Stern, Barrie, 97
Stichting-Reprorecht, 52

Tagler, John, 73,142-143
Technical Services, Public Services cooperation with, 149-151
TECHNO-COM/CD-ROM Teleconference, 109
Texaco, 59
Tolbert, Jack, 157

UKMARC, 134
Unique Copy Shop, 59
United States Newspaper Project, 137
Universal Copyright Convention, 52-53
University of Bradford, 97,98
University of Georgia Libraries, 146-147
University libraries/universities. *See also* names of specific institutions
  Copyright Clearance Center site licensing of, 23,53-54,69
  copyright infringements by, 59
  electronic journal access by, 73-83
  photocopying copyright problems, 63-71
University Microfilms, 88
URICA, 166
USMARC, 109,134,135,137

Format for Holdings and Locations, 145-147

Veliotes, Nicholas, 59-60,61-62
Vendor
 foreign journal pricing and, 141
 librarian/publisher relationship, 125,126, 127,128-129,130-131

VG Wort, 52
Videocassette
 copyright law and, 66
 as multiple version, 136,137

Willmering, Bill, 161,162
Wiltse, Helen Citron, 170
Winter, Harvey, 59-60
Winthrop College Library, 166

For Product Safety Concerns and Information please contact our EU
representative GPSR@taylorandfrancis.com
Taylor & Francis Verlag GmbH, Kaufingerstraße 24, 80331 München, Germany

www.ingramcontent.com/pod-product-compliance
Lightning Source LLC
Chambersburg PA
CBHW052120300426
44116CB00010B/1742